# PEACEFAKERS,
# PEACEBREAKERS,
*and*
# PEACEMAKERS

# KEN SANDE
## & KAY MOORE

**HANNIBAL BOOKS**
www.hannibalbooks.com

# To order copies of
# *Peacefakers, Peacebreakers, and Peacemakers*

*Member Book, Leader Guide*, video, trade book, or *Leader Kit*

**Contact:**
**Hannibal Books**
**P.O. Box 461592**
**Garland, Texas 75046**

**Phone: 1-800-747-0738**
**Visit: *www.hannibalbooks.com***
**Fax: 1-888-252-3022**
**Email: *hannibalbooks@earthlink.net***

Copyright Peacemaker Ministries, 2005
All Rights Reserved
Printed in the United States of America
by Versa Press, Inc., East Peoria IL
Cover design by Greg Crull

Unless otherwise noted, all Scripture quotations are taken from Holy Bible, New International Version, copyright 1973, 1978, 1984 by International Bible Society

Library of Congress Control Number: 2004111004
ISBN 0-929292-95-2

# TABLE OF CONTENTS

# Preface

People basically respond to conflict in three ways. **Peace-fakers** try to avoid conflict by pretending problems don't exist or by pulling away from difficult relationships. **Peacebreakers** try to intimidate or overpower opponents through forceful arguments, threats, or aggressive action. **Peacemakers** work toward genuine agreement and attempt to restore broken relationships by treating others as they would like to be treated themselves.

Peacefakers and peacebreakers experience many superficial or broken relationships. They rarely have an effective witness for Christ. In contrast, peacemakers usually enjoy lasting relationships. More importantly, they send a credible message that Jesus Christ is real, that He has saved us from our sins, and that He delights to give us the power to imitate His love and forgiveness toward others—even those who have done us great wrong.

By God's grace, this study can help you throw off life-long habits of peacefaking and peacebreaking. You can learn how to be an effective peacemaker in your family, church, and workplace. As you learn how to live out the gospel of Christ in daily conflicts and to apply the practical peacemaking principles He has given to us in His Word, you will have the joy of being used by God to restore broken relationships and to help people know and trust in the love of Christ. You have His Word on this: He, Himself, promised, "Blessed are the peacemakers!" (Matt. 5:9).

Ken Sande
President
Peacemaker Ministries

# First Six Weeks

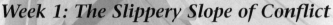

# *Week 1: The Slippery Slope of Conflict*

**1. A time I wish I'd known more about how to resolve conflict:**

_workplace issues_

**2. Four "G's" of biblical peacemaking**

1. G _lorify God_ (verse: _I Cor 10:31_)
2. G _et the plog out of your own_ (verse: _Matt 7:5_ )
3. G _ently restore_ (verse: _Gal 6:1_ )
4. G _o and be Reconciled_ (verse: _Matt 5:24_)

Put a star beside the "G" that is most difficult for you.

**3. Take a stab at defining conflict. What's your definition?**

_difference in opinions/purpose_

**4. Four basic causes of conflict**

1.
    _Misunderstandings from poor communication_

    (Josh. 22:10-34)

2.
    _Differences in values, goals, etc_

    (Acts 15:39; 1 Cor. 12:12-31) _(Personal Differences)_

10

3. _Limited (resources)_
(Gen. 13:1-12)

4. _Sinful attitudes, habits leading_
(Jas. 4:1-12) _to sinful attitudes_

Go back and put a star beside the one of the four causes that you believe most often categorizes the conflicts you face.

*diagram pg 139*

**5. Match the type of response listed in the first column with the description of it in the second column.**

**Ways people respond to conflict**

_2_ a. reconciliation -m

_3_ b. murder -b

_10_ c. arbitration -m

_4_ d. denial -f

_6_ e. litigation -b

_5_ f. assault -b

_8_ g. suicide -f

_9_ h. overlooking -m

_10_ i. mediation -m

_11_ j. accountability -m

_7_ k. flight -f

_12_ l. negotiation -m

**Description**

1. outside people meet with parties to help them communicate and explore solutions
2. resolving issues through confession, loving correction, forgiveness
3. hating or killing someone
4. pretending a conflict does not exist
5. using force or intimidation to get your way
6. taking someone to court
7. escaping conflict by running away
8. escaping the situation by taking one's own life
9. quietly and deliberately choosing to let go of an offense
10. asking one or more objective outside people to meet with parties and decide the matter
11. church leaders formally intervene and hold people accountable to Scripture
12. a cooperative bargaining process in which two people seek to reach a settlement satisfying needs of each side

Go back to the exercise and mark each response with one of the following designations: pf—peacefaking; pb—peacebreaking; pm—peacemaking.

**6. As you watch "Gossiping about Gossip" from *Peacemaker Parables*, answer these questions:**

a. Who was contributing to the conflict? How?

b. Which Slippery Slope responses were various people using?

c. How did these people make the conflict better or worse?

d. Which response should Laura use?

**7. Responses to Conflict in the Bible chart (see chart on page 12).**

**8. Which of the Slippery Slope responses are you most likely to use when you are faced with a conflict? Does it usually help or hinder a resolution?**

overlook, deny, confront
depends on situation

**9. If you were to pray for God to help you change one aspect of the way you respond to conflict, what would it be? Write that prayer below. Pray it silently as a request to God.** be less argumentative / be more open to others opinions.

**10. For further study:**
a. Read *The Peacemaker* (3d ed.) (pp. 21-30).
b. Complete "Responses to Conflict in the Bible" (p. 12).
c. Do the week-1 Daily Devotionals, adapted from *The Peacemaker* (pp. 13-17).

# Responses to Conflict in the Bible

**Indicate which Slippery Slope response to conflict was used and whether it was wise ("+") or foolish/sinful ("-"):**

1. Abraham's response to the friction between Sarai and Hagar (Gen. 16:6).
2. Hagar's response to Sarai's persecution (Gen. 16:6-8).
3. Joseph's response when Potiphar's wife tried to seduce him (Gen. 39:11-12).
4. Potiphar's wife's response when Joseph spurned her advances (Gen. 39:13-18).
5. Pharaoh's response to the plagues God brought upon him (Ex. 7:1-12:36).
6. Saul's response to David when he won the hearts of the people (1 Sam. 18:1-16).
7. David's response to Saul's attempts to kill him (1 Sam. 19:9-12).
8. Solomon's response to the dispute over the prostitute's baby (1 Kings 3:16-28).
9. Daniel's response to the command to eat unclean food (Dan. 1:8-16).
10. Jonah's response to God's command to go to Nineveh (Jonah 1:3).
11. Joseph's response when Herod was searching for Jesus (Matt. 2:13-15).
12. Judas Iscariot's response to the inner conflict he felt after betraying the Lord (Matt. 27:5).
13. The Corinthians' response to legal conflicts with one another (1 Cor. 6:1-8).
14. The apostles' response to the conflict about distributing food (Acts 6:1-7).
15. Barnabas' response to the conflict between Saul and the apostles (Acts 9:26-28).
16. Peter's response when Jewish Christians complained about teaching Gentiles (Acts 11:1-18).
17. The Philippian slave owners' response when Paul delivered the woman from spiritual bondage (Acts 16:16-22).
18. Paul's response to Peter's support of circumcision group (Acts 15:1-29; Gal. 2:11-21).
19. Paul's response when charged with crimes in Jerusalem (Acts 24:1-26:32).
20. The Pharisees' response to Jesus.

Bonus: God's response to our sin (the gospel).

# Day 1. The Farm and the Family

*Today's verse: How good and pleasant it is when brothers live together in unity! (Ps. 133:1).*

"Don't try to come in!" Frank yelled through the door. "I have a bat. I'll hit anyone who comes in."

"Come on. Open the door, Frank!" Joe responded from the porch. "We just want to talk."

"This is getting out of control," Jenny said, tugging at Joe's arm. "Let's ask our lawyer to talk with Frank."

"But the realtor and the buyer are on their way. We'll lose the deal if they can't get in to look at the house."

"We'll lose even more if Frank goes after them with a bat! I'm going to call and postpone the meeting until we can do something with Frank."

"OK, but I won't let him hold up this sale forever," Joe replied angrily. "You've got two days to get him out of here, Jenny. After that, I'll come back with my own bat. John and Matt will be happy to join me."

Jenny felt trapped among her four brothers, who were fighting over the farm. Born disabled, Frank was confined to home all his life and in their mother's care. As Mom's health failed, Frank looked after her. When she finally died after a stroke, Frank's world collapsed.

Earlier, the parents had established a trust to provide for Frank. They had left the farm equally to their other four children. With both parents now deceased, Joe, John, and Matt wanted to sell quickly. Frank was terrified of moving from the family home. Heated arguments had ensued. Jenny needed the money as badly as her brothers did, but she hated to evict Frank. Her other brothers seemed oblivious to his fears and wanted to push ahead with the sale. What should Jenny do?

*Father, help me be sensitive to those around me. Help me to look beyond my own interests and exhibit compassion.*

## Day 2. What Would Jesus Do?

*Today's verse: So whether you eat or drink or whatever you do, do it all for the glory of God (1 Cor. 10:31).*

While Jenny contemplated her family's quandary, she remembered that her pastor recently had attended a biblical peacemaking seminar. After a brief call, the pastor agreed to meet that night with Jenny, Joe, John, and Matt.

"Look, Pastor," Joe said, "I'm only asking that we honor Mom's wishes. She and Dad years ago set up a trust for Frank and told the rest of us to divide the farm. As executor for her estate, I'm legally responsible for honoring her will. Frank may hate to move out, but he can settle into a nice apartment complex in town."

"But it could kill him," Jenny begged. "If we force Frank out, he'll lose everything familiar to him."

Matt injected. "So, do we sit around until he dies years from now, then divide up the property? I have two kids in college. Mom would want to see them helped. I agree with Joe; we should honor Mom's will and follow the law."

"I appreciate your respect for your mother and for the law," said Pastor Barry, "but you have another consideration. All of you profess to be Christians. What's the difference between how you are dealing with this and the way a good atheist would deal with it?"

After several moments of awkward silence, Pastor Barry elaborated, "What matters more in this situation—to get your money as soon as possible, as most people would, or to demonstrate to your brother Christ's love? How can you treat each other in a way that shows the power of the gospel in each of your lives?"

"That sounds good, Pastor," Joe replied, "but I don't see how religion applies to this problem."

"Then let's pray together now and ask God to show you how you can solve this conflict in a way that honors Him and fulfills your parents' wishes."

*Help me, Lord, to respond to conflict in a way that is so different from the world's way that others will see Jesus' love working in me.*

## Day 3. Demonstrating God's Power

*Today's verse: Greater love has no one than this, that he lay down his life for his friends (John 15:13).*

God answered Jenny's family's prayers in a way no one expected.

Three weeks later, the entire extended family gathered in the banquet room of a local restaurant. Jenny had somehow overcome Frank's fears and persuaded him to leave the house and join the family for dinner.

Twelve nephews and nieces watched with rapt attention as Frank entered the room and nervously sat down at one end of the table.

Joe, as the eldest son, asked for everyone's attention. He began: "Frank, our family is gathered together today to honor you. For the past 10 years you devoted yourself to caring for Mom. Today we want to present you with this special plaque. It says, 'To our brother, Frank, the best of all sons, who cared for our mother with selfless love and undying devotion. Your companionship filled her life with joy and delight and was a constant reminder to her of the love of God. With deepest gratitude to a wonderful brother, from Joe, John, Jenny, and Matt.'"

Tears welled up in Frank's eyes as Joe handed him the plaque.

But Joe hadn't addressed the situation about the farm. Frank couldn't help wondering if something were behind this decision to honor him in such a lavish way. Although he was grateful for the tribute, he sat silent in the presence of his siblings. He waited for the other shoe to drop.

*Help me remember, Lord, that Your Word says that the greatest love one can show is to lay down his or her life for a friend. Help me be willing to live sacrificially and to be caring with all whom I encounter.*

## Day 4. "There Is a God!"

*Today's verse: You show that you are a letter from Christ . . .
written not with ink but with the Spirit of the living God, not
on tablets of stone but on tablets of human hearts (2 Cor. 3:3).*

While Frank pondered what ultimately would happen
to him and to his home, Joe handed him an envelope.

"Frank," Joe went on, "in appreciation for all you did
for Mom, we want to give you this gift. This agreement
that we have all signed gives you a life estate in the farm-
house. That means you will be able to stay there for as
long as you live. A buyer is willing to purchase the rest of
the farm land. Ownership of the house eventually will
pass to our children. But as long as you want to live there,
we want you to know that it is your home."

As Frank clutched the envelope, months of uncertainty
and fear gave way to sobs of relief and gratitude. Joe
hugged his brother for the first time in years.

As Joe's teen-aged son observed this scene, he leaned
toward his sister and whispered, "Maybe there is a God,
after all. Dad never would have done this on his own."

*How I desire, Lord, to be a walking testimony for you! Help me
to remember that sometimes all that others know of You is what
they see in my words and deeds.*

## Day 5. Finding God's Solution

*Today's verse: Since, then, you have been raised with Christ, set your hearts on things above, where Christ is seated at the right hand of God. Set your minds on things above, not on earthly things (Col. 3:1-2).*

When someone mistreats or opposes us, we instinctively justify ourselves and do everything we can to get our way. This selfish attitude usually leads to impulsive decisions that only worsen things.

If Jenny's other brothers had carried out their desires to evict Frank or to intrude on him with a bat, as one threatened, a family breach that could have been irreparable likely would have ensued.

The gospel of Jesus Christ provides the way out of this downward spiral. When we remember what Jesus did for us on the cross, our blinding self-absorption can be replaced with a liberating desire to draw attention to the goodness and power of God.

Focusing on God is the key to resolving conflict constructively. Jenny's pastor was wise to recommend that the siblings consider their responsibilities as Christians and to pray for God's unfailing wisdom in the situation.

When we remember His mercy and draw on His strength, we invariably see things more clearly and respond more wisely. In doing so, we can find far better solutions to our problems. The ultimate solution that Joe outlined for Frank at the family gathering was creative, reasonable, and a win-win outcome for all parties involved.

At the same time, we can, as Joe did, demonstrate to others that God indeed exists and that He delights in helping us to do things we never could have done on our own.

*God, help me remember that you care far more about helping me find Your solutions to my problems than even I do. Help me to turn to you with every situation confronting me.*

## Week 2: Conflict Provides Opportunities

**1. One way that I tried to remember to act as a Christian would during a conflict (preferably during the past week):**

_____

**2. Think of a personality or temperament difference between you and someone to whom you relate (spouse, child, co-worker, etc.). Describe how that difference can actually benefit you and the other person.**

_____
_____
_____

**3. Three opportunities in conflict:**
   **I. Glorify God**
      a. Trust God.
      b. Obey God.
      c. Imitate God.
      d. Acknowledge God.

**Describe a time you responded to conflict in a way that might have appeared "unnatural" to others but which you used as an opportunity to testify to God's power.**

_____
_____
_____

## II. Serve Others
   a. Help an opponent find better solutions.
   b. Carry an opponent's burdens.
   c. Help others learn where they have erred.
   d. Provide opportunities to introduce others to Christ.
   e. Encourage by your example.

**As your leader describes these means of service through conflict (just listed), put a star by one way that you will commit to use to serve others in the days ahead.**

## III. Grow to Be like Christ
   a. _____
      (2 Cor. 12:8-9)
   b. _____
      (Ps. 119:67)
   c._____
      (2 Cor. 5:17)

**4. As you watch "The Walls Come Tumbling Down" from *Peacemaker Parables*, answer these questions:**

   a. What Slippery Slope response was the father using?

   b. What Slippery Slope response was Helen using?

   c. What Slippery Slope response was Megan using?

   d. How could the family turn this conflict into an opportunity to glorify God, serve other people, and grow to be like Christ?

## 5. Recurring Themes of Peace in the Bible

a. _____

(Rom. 15:33; 2 Cor. 13:11; Phil. 4:9; Heb. 13:20;
Judg. 6:24)

b. _____

(Lev. 26:6; Num. 6:24-26; Judg. 5:31; Ps. 29:11; 119:165;
Prov. 16:7; Mic. 4:1-4; Gal. 6:16)

c. _____

(Ps. 34:14; Jer. 29:7; Rom. 14:19; 1 Cor. 7:15;
2 Cor. 13:11; Col. 3:15; 1 Thess. 5:13; Heb. 12:14)

d._____

(Num. 25:12; Isa. 54:10; Ezek. 34:25; 37:26; Mal. 2:5)

e. _____

(Judg. 6:23; 1 Sam. 16:5; Luke 24:36; 1 Sam. 1:17;
2 Kings 5:19; Luke 7:50; 8:48; Rom. 1:7; 15:13;
Gal. 1:3; 2 Thess. 3:16)

**6. Think about which of the three opportunities in conflict—to glorify God, to serve others, and to grow to be like Christ—is the easiest and which one is the most difficult for you. Write your answer.**

**7. If you were to pray for God to help you change one way in which you view conflict so you can begin seeing it as an opportunity, what would it be? Write that prayer below. Pray it silently as a request to God.**

**8. For further study:**
a. Read *The Peacemaker* (3d ed.) (pp. 31-40).
b. Complete "Recurring Themes of Peace in the Bible" (p. 20).
c. Do the week-2 Daily Devotionals, adapted from *The Peacemaker* (pp. 21-25).
d. Complete "If You Are Presently Involved in a Conflict" (pp. 26-27).

## Devotional readings for Week 2

# Day 1. An Invitation to Church

*Today's verse: Therefore, since we have been justified through faith, we have peace with God through our Lord Jesus Christ, through whom we have gained access by faith into this grace in which we now stand (Rom. 5:1-2).*

When I was in law school, I invited a friend to attend church with me. Cindy was struggling in her spiritual life and was disillusioned with her church. Thinking she might benefit from my church, I invited her to worship with me one Sunday.

Moments after we took our seats, Pastor Erbele surprised everyone. He called for the attention of the congregation and asked one of the elders to step to the podium.

Suddenly I remembered that the pastor and the elder, whose name was Kent, had had a heated discussion during the previous week's Sunday-school class.

"Oh, no!" I thought. "The pastor is going to rebuke Kent in front of the whole church." I was terribly embarrassed as I thought what a terrible impression this would make on Cindy, who already had some negative feelings about church in general.

"As most of you know," Pastor Erbele went on, "Kent and I had an argument during Sunday school last week. Our emotions got out of hand. We said some things that we should have discussed in private."

My stomach sank even further. "Of all the days to bring someone to church," I moaned to myself. "Why did I pick this one?" I was sure this incident would discourage Cindy totally and destroy her respect for my pastor. I wondered how I would ever face Cindy after this.

*Help me, dear God, to learn to put my ultimate trust in You and not in other people.*

## Day 2. A United Front

*Today's verse: May the God who gives endurance and encouragement give you a spirit of unity among yourselves as you follow Christ Jesus, so that with one heart and mouth you may glorify the God and Father of our Lord Jesus Christ (Rom. 15:5-6).*

I'm glad I didn't decide to leave the church in my embarrassment when Pastor Erbele began speaking about his dispute with Kent during last week's Sunday-school time.

As he continued with his comments to the congregation, my pastor put his arm around Kent's shoulders and went on. "We want you to know that Kent and I met later that afternoon to resolve our differences. By God's grace, we began to understand each other better. We were fully reconciled, but we need to tell you how sorry we are for disrupting the unity of this fellowship. We ask you to forgive us for the poor example we gave last week."

Kent then made a similar statement to what the pastor had said. Many eyes filled with tears at these comments. Unfortunately, I was so worried about what Cindy was thinking that I missed the significance of what was happening.

Making a nervous comment to Cindy, I opened the hymnal to our first song and hoped she would forget about the comments just made from the pulpit.

The rest of the service was a blur; before long I was driving her home. We made light conversation for a few minutes, but eventually Cindy referred to what occurred. "I still can't believe what your pastor did this morning," she said. "I've never seen a minister do something like that."

I held my breath. I didn't know whether she was disgusted or impressed with what she had seen.

*Lord, you are in control over all things. Move me to give you total charge over all my life.*

# Day 3. A Surprise Ending

*Today's verse: Live such good lives among the pagans that, though they accuse you of doing wrong, they may see your good deeds and glorify God on the day he visits us (1 Pet. 2:12).*

I was apprehensive about what Cindy would say next about my pastor. She went on:

"Could I return to your church next week?"

I was shocked. "You're serious? You want to visit my church again?"

"I've never been so impressed," she went on. "These men were open and honest about their quarrel. Then they made an effort to patch it up and to let everyone know they were reconciled. They came across as real people who took their faith seriously."

During subsequent visits, Cindy listened intently when my pastor spoke. Having seen the power of the gospel in his life, she was eager to hear about the salvation and freedom she could experience by trusting in Jesus. Within a month, she committed her life to Christ and made our church her spiritual home.

When I brought Cindy to church that first morning, I had hoped to impress her with the friendliness of my fellow members and with my pastor's preaching. But God had a far more effective plan in mind. He exposed the embarrassing conflict in our midst and showed that my pastor was far from perfect.

Then, against this humbling backdrop of our imperfections, he revealed his grace by demonstrating the reconciling power of Jesus Christ in our midst.

By moving two men to breathe grace in the midst of conflict, God brought Cindy into His Kingdom.

*Dear God, help me remember that others are watching how I act and are more likely to believe in You if I behave in a Christlike fashion.*

## Day 4. Watching for the Real Enemy

*Today's verse: Our struggle is not against flesh and blood, but against the rulers, against the authorities, against the powers of this dark world and against the spiritual forces of evil in the heavenly realms (Eph. 6:12).*

As you just saw in the story of Pastor Erbele and Kent, peace and unity are essential to an effective Christian witness. You can be sure that someone exists who will do all he can to promote conflict and division among believers.

Satan promotes conflict in many ways. Among other things, he tempts us so we give in to greed and dishonesty (Acts 5:3), he deceives us as to what will make us happy (2 Tim. 2:25-26), and he takes advantage of unresolved anger (Eph. 4:26-27).

Worst of all, Satan uses false teachers to propagate values and philosophies that encourage selfishness and stimulate controversy (1 Tim. 4:1-3).

Here are some expressions that often reflect the devil's lies and influence:

*"Look out for Number One."*

*"Don't get mad; get even."*

*"I'll forgive you, but I won't forget."*

Satan prefers that we do not recognize his role in our conflicts. For example, Pastor Erbele and Kent could have ignored Satan's attacks and blamed each other in the dispute. They could have been blinded to what Satan was trying to do to disrupt the congregation through their quarrel. As long as we see other people as our only adversaries and focus our attacks on them, we will give no thought to guarding against our most dangerous enemy.

Paul warns about this in our verse for today. He warns for us to be aware of Satan's goals and to guard against his influences.

*Help me be alert, dear Lord, to the ways Satan tries to trip me up in my efforts to maintain peace.*

# Day 5. A Management Opportunity

*Today's verse: He has showed you, O man, what is good. And what does the Lord require of you? To act justly and to love mercy and to walk humbly with your God (Mic. 6:8).*

We often hear the word "stewardship" as it applies to giving to the church. But have you ever thought of being a "good steward" of conflict? *Stewarding* conflict is an amazingly effective approach to peacemaking

When Jesus talked about managing something, he usually referred to a servant whose master had entrusted him with certain resources and responsibilities (Luke 12:42). When we are in conflict, God gives us a management opportunity. His Word tells us how. We are to be:

*Motivated*—You are to overcome selfish, short-sighted attitudes and to give yourself to serving and honoring God.

*Informed*—The Bible gives us detailed, practical instructions on how to deal with problems in daily life (2 Tim. 3:16-17). When you know the Bible, you are more likely to respond to problems God's way (Deut. 29:29).

*Dependent*—When a conflict pushes you beyond your resources, turn to godly advisers in the church. Look for people who will love you enough to be honest with you about the correct way for you to live.

*Faithful*—God knows that you cannot control other people, so He will not hold you responsible for a conflict's ultimate outcome. Success, in God's eyes, depends only on whether you sought His guidance, obeyed His commands, and wisely used the resources he has given you. Were you faithful?

*Father, I pray that You'll help me look on conflict as a chance to serve You. I pray You'll find me a faithful steward who managed my opportunities well.*

## If You Are Presently Involved in a Conflict

Answering these questions will help you apply to your situation the principles presented in this week's study.

1. Briefly summarize your dispute as you perceive it, placing events in chronological order as much as possible. In particular, describe what you have done to resolve the dispute.

2. Which response to conflict (from the Slippery Slope diagram) have you used to resolve this dispute? How has your response made the situation better or worse?

3. What have been your primary goals as you've tried to resolve this dispute?

4. From this point on, how could you glorify God through this conflict? Specifically, how could you please and honor God in this situation and bring praise to Jesus by showing that He has saved you and is changing you?

5. How could you serve others through this conflict?

6. How could you grow to be more like Christ through this conflict?

7. On what have you relied for guidance in this situation: your feelings and personal opinions about what is right, or the careful study and application of what is taught in the Bible? On what will you rely in the future?

8. How could you use the resources God has provided (the Bible, the Holy Spirit, or other Christians) to deal with these struggles?

9. If God were to evaluate this conflict after it is over, how would you like Him to complete these sentences:

"I am pleased that you did not . . .."

"I am pleased that you . . .."

10. Go on record with the Lord by writing a prayer based on the principles this chapter teaches.

## *Week 3: Conflict Starts in the Heart*

**1. Think of a person whom you have observed dealing with a conflict in a Christlike way. This conflict may have been recent or may have happened years ago. Describe what impressed you about how the person acted in the midst of the conflict.**

_____

_____

_____

**2. The progression of an idol—**

I _desire_

I _demand_

I _judge_

I _punish_

An "idol" is anything apart from God that controls us and that we depend on to be happy, fulfilled, or secure (Luke 12:29; Jas. 4:1-3).

**3. Use these X-ray questions to identify desires that may have become idols.**

- What preoccupies me? What is the first thing on my mind in the morning and the last thing on my mind at night?

  _work_

  _____

- What goes in this blank—"If only _____
  _____, I would be happy, fulfilled, and
  secure"?

- What is something I want so much that I would
  disappoint or hurt others in order to have it?

  _____

- When a certain desire is not met, do I feel frustration,
  anxiety, resentment, bitterness, anger, depression?
  __*frustration*_____

**4. Look up the Scripture beside each means that God
has provided you for your deliverance from specific
idols. Fill in the missing word in each sentence. Put a
star by one of these ways you will commit to using, by
God's grace, in the days ahead.**
  - Use the ___*Bible*____ to shine its Word of
    truth into your heart (Heb. 4:12). As you diligently
    study it, it will reveal your idolatrous desires and
    show you how to love and worship God with all
    that you are.
  - Be sensitive to the __*Holy Spirit*__ who convicts
    you and helps you pursue a godly life.
    (Phil. 2:13).
  - Be consistently involved in your __*Church*___,
    where spiritually mature Christian brothers and
    sisters can teach us, encourage us, and hold us
    accountable for our idols (Gal. 6:1) and where we
    can sit under godly preaching to better understand
    God's Word.

**5. As you watch "Repentance" from *Peacemaker
Parables*, answer these questions:**

  a. What got things off to a bad start in the conflict?

  _____

  b. What Slippery Slope responses did the couple use?

  _____

c. What was the turning point in the conversation?

_____

d. What desires seem to have turned into idols?

_____

**6. Steps to Replacing Idol Worship with Worship of the True God**

a. <u>acknowledge sin & confess</u>
(1 John 1:8-10; Ps. 51:17; Isa. 66:2b)

b. <u>fear God</u>
(Prov. 1:7; Matt. 10:28; Ps. 130:3-4)

c. <u>love the Lord + seek him</u>
(Matt. 22:37; Ps. 34:10; Matt. 6:33; Ps. 73:25-26)

d. <u>commit to God</u>
(Ps. 118:3; Ps. 37:5-6; 2 Pet. 1:3-4)

e. <u>have joy in God</u>
(Ps. 37:4; Ps. 71:3; Phil. 4:4; 1 Thess. 5:16-17)

**7. Describe a time when a godly person helped you see that a good desire had grown into a controlling idol and was taking first place in your life.**


**8. Write a brief prayer in which you ask God to help you guard your heart against desires that grow into demands and cause conflict. Then pray this silently as a request to God.**

**9. For further study:**

    a. Read *The Peacemaker* (3d ed.) (pp. 100-115).

    b. Complete "Steps to Replacing Idol Worship with Worship of the True God" (p. 30).

    c. Do the week-3 Daily Devotionals, adapted from *The Peacemaker* (pp. 32-36).

    d. Complete "If You Are Presently Involved in a Conflict" (pp. 37-38).

Devotional Readings for Week 3

# Day 1. A Not-So-Serene Sunday

*Today's verse: What causes fights and quarrels among you? Don't they come from your desires that battle within you? (Jas. 4:1).*

All I wanted was a little peace and quiet when I arrived home from a long day at the office. But I was not getting it. My children, Megan and Jeff, had been trying to control each other all week. Their mother was exhausted with their constant friction. Instead of resolving their quarrels with her usual calmness, Corlette found herself resorting to sharp words and to threats such as "Wait until your father gets home!"

So, instead of walking through the door and finding smiling children and a serene, affectionate wife, I found nothing but sullen faces, irritable voices, and the general sense that I had walked into a war zone.

Each evening Corlette and I had worked to break the cycle of conflict, but it would start again in a day or two. By Sunday morning I was feeling frustrated and resentful toward my children.

Corlette had gone to church early that morning to meet with some women. I was following 30 minutes later with the kids. As we approached the car, a new conflict erupted.

"It's my turn to sit in the front seat!"

"No, you got to yesterday!"

"Well, you shouldn't sit there anyway. You're so small, the airbag could kill you."

"I don't care. I'm not sitting in the back seat."

The conflict was unending. How was I, as their father, to resolve this ongoing battle that threatened to rage all the way to church and disrupt our worship time?

*Lord, give me wisdom when I find myself in the midst of a family conflict. Help me be an example of Your peace.*

# Day 2. The Heart of the Conflict

*Today's verse: You want something but don't get it. You kill and covet, but you cannot have what you want. You quarrel and fight. You do not have, because you do not ask God. When you ask, you do not receive, because you ask with wrong motives, that you may spend what you get on your pleasures (Jas. 4:2-3).*

As my children railed at each other, a new voice entered the exchange.

"Be quiet!" I shouted. Then, pointing to each child in turn, "You get in the back seat right now; you get in the front seat. I don't want to hear another word from either of you."

Climbing into the car myself, I gave vent to the anger that had been building in me all week. I even adjusted the rearview mirror so I could glare at Megan as I lectured her in the back seat.

Among other things, I told them I was very angry at the way they had behaved all week and that I was now going to make things miserable for them.

When I finally paused to take a breath, Jeffrey saw his opening.

"Daddy," he asked meekly. "do you think you should pray to Jesus and ask Him if it's rightful anger?"

The Holy Spirit must have guided his words, because they instantly cut me to the core. I saw an empty parking lot and pulled in. Before I had even turned off the ignition, I knew what I had to say. Turning to our children, I went to the heart of our conflict.

*I pray, dear Father, that you'll keep me open to the promptings of the Holy Spirit. I realize that sometimes these promptings can occur in my conversations with others.*

## Day 3. When Idols Rule

*Today's verse: If someone is caught in a sin, you who are spiritual should restore him gently (Gal. 6:1).*

The two passages from James 4:1-2, which appear in the day-1 and day-2 vignettes, describe with painful accuracy my behavior that Sunday morning. They also sum up my family's behavior all that week.

James specifically applies a fundamental principle Jesus taught in Matthew 15:19: "Out of the heart come evil thoughts, murder, adultery, sexual immorality, theft, false testimony, slander." Our heart is the wellspring of all our thoughts, words, and actions. Therefore, it is also the source of our conflicts (Luke 12:13-15).

These passages describe the root cause of conflict: unmet desires in our hearts. When we want something and believe that we will not be satisfied unless we get it, that desire starts to control us. If others fail to meet our desires, we fight to get our own way.

If God-centered desires had dominated my heart that week, my attitude toward my disobedient children would have been characterized by God's discipline toward me: "The Lord is compassionate and gracious, slow to anger abounding in love" (Ps. 103:8). As I drew on God's grace, my actions would have been in line with the corrective guidelines found in Galatians 6:1, as seen in today's verse. My discipline still could have been direct and firm, but it also would have been wrapped in gentleness and love.

But this was not how I was feeling or acting. My behavior throughout the week was marred by an increasing coolness and smoldering resentment toward my children. On Sunday morning my frustration had finally overflowed. Clearly, my desire for peace and quiet for the sake of my own comfort was ruling me. I was serving this idol instead of my God. What was I to do now?

*I pray You'll help me, Father, to discern whether an idol is controlling me when I want something I cannot have.*

# Day 4. From Bitterness to Joy

*Today's verse: Those who seek the Lord lack no good thing (Ps. 34:10).*

As you learn to delight more in God, you will feel less need to find happiness, fulfillment, and security in the things of the world.

By God's grace, the influence of idolatry and its resulting conflict in your life can be steadily diminished. From worshiping the one true God you can find the intimacy and security that you desire.

This is what happened the morning I blew up at my children. The Holy Spirit graciously exposed my idolatry through my son's insightful question, "Daddy, do you think you should pray to Jesus and ask Him if it's rightful anger?" Even as I pulled into the empty parking lot, God revealed the answer in my heart: my anger was anything but "rightful." It sprang from my worshiping an idol of comfort and convenience.

I confessed this to my children and asked them to forgive me for my answer and harsh words. They responded with hugs of forgiveness and confessed that they, too, had been serving idols that week.

The Lord lovingly enabled us to cast down the gods of conflict and remind each other that the true God is so much better than the idols we had been serving.

We were a few minutes late to church that morning, but our worship was more sincere, joyful, and exhilarating than it had been for a long time.

*Dear Lord, help me to feel content in You, knowing that You are all I ever need.*

## Day 5. On the Alert

*Today's verse: The one who sows to please his sinful nature, from that nature will reap destruction; the one who sows to please the Spirit, from the Spirit will reap eternal life (Gal. 6:8).*

How can we be on the alert for idols that threaten to distract and derail us? Using a journal to keep track of discoveries such as the one I made helps you identify patterns and steadily go after specific idols.

Pray daily that God will keep your idols from influencing your life by making you miserable when you give in to them. An accountability partner is a good idea; this can be your spouse or a trusted, Christian friend. Describe your idols to that person. Ask him or her to pray for you and to lovingly approach you when signs appear that the idol still controls you.

Realize that idols are masters of change and disguise. As soon as you gain a victory over a particular demand or form of punishment, your idol can reappear in a related form, with a new justification. If you are dealing with an idol that is difficult to conquer, seek counsel and support from some other spiritually mature advisor.

If someone told you that you had a deadly cancer that could take your life if you did not get treatment, you would pursue the most rigorous treatment available. You do have a cancer—a cancer of the soul. It is called sin and idolatry. A priceless cure is freely available—the gospel of Jesus Christ. It is administered through the Word, the Spirit, and the church. The more vigorously you avail yourself of these means of grace, the greater effect they will have in delivering you from the idols that plague your soul and disrupt your relationships.

God delights in delivering us from our slavery to idols and enables us to find true freedom, fulfillment, and security in His love and provision. As we break free from the desires fueling our conflicts, we can resolve seemingly hopeless disputes and become better peacemakers.

*Lord, help me remove from my life anything that keeps me from realizing my dependence on You.*

## If You Are Presently Involved in a Conflict

**Answering these questions will help you apply to your situation the principles presented in this week's study.**

1. Work backward through the progression of an idol to identify the desires that control your heart. Ask yourself these questions:
   a. How am I punishing others?

   b. How am I judging others?

   c. What am I demanding to have?

   d. What is the root desire of that demand?

2. What makes you think that you need or deserve to have any of these desires satisfied?

3. In order to more clearly identify your idols (desires turned into demands), ask yourself these questions:
   a. With what am I preoccupied? (What is the first thing on my mind in the morning and/or the last thing at night?)

   b. How would I fill in this blank—"If only _____, then I would be happy, fulfilled, and secure"?

   c. What do I want to preserve or avoid at any cost?

   d. Where do I put my trust?

   e. What do I fear?

   f. When a certain desire is not met, do I feel frustration, anxiety, resentment, bitterness, anger, or depression?

g. Do I desire something so much that I am willing to disappoint or hurt others in order to have it?

4. How are your expectations of others magnifying your demands on them and your disappointment in their failure to meet your desires?

5. How are you judging those who do not meet your desires? Are you feeling indignation, condemnation, bitterness, resentment, or anger?

6. How are you punishing those who do not meet your desires?

7. What has God done to deliver you from your idols? What can you do to receive this deliverance?

8. How can you cultivate a more passionate love for and worship of God?

9. Go on record with the Lord by writing a prayer based on the principles this chapter teaches.

## Week 4: Confession Brings Freedom

**1. Think back to a conflict you have had with another person. Describe one way you contributed to that conflict.**

_____

_____

**2. After you read the following case studies, put a check beside the one that demonstrates true repentance.**

_____ a. Mary approached Todd to apologize about their argument last week. She told Todd, "I'm sorry I yelled at you, but if you hadn't kept my book so long that I couldn't study for my test, I wouldn't have reacted."

_____ b. Michael told Dad, "I can't go back to school for two days because the teacher said I spoke rudely to her. Boy, I sure hate missing the pep rally because of this suspension."

_____ c. Angelina told April, "I'm sorry I hurt you when I broke my promise to you not to tell about your parents' separation. I've felt sad for days since God put it on my heart what a poor friend I've been to you."

_____ d. Lance left the following message on Heather's voice mail: "You made me so mad when you forgot my birthday. I know I've forgotten yours yours at times, too, but I dropped at least a dozen hints. You deserved it when I stood you up today."

## 3. Ways We Sin

### (1) Using Our Tongues as Weapons

Below, match the type of damage inflicted (left-hand column) with the definition (right-hand column)

| | |
|---|---|
| _____ a. slander (Lev. 19:16) | 1. includes lying, exaggeration, telling half-truths, destroying trust |
| _____ b. falsehood (Prov. 24:28) | 2. careless, critical, meaningless words not designed to benefit others |
| _____ c. reckless words (Prov. 12:8) | 3. when others feel we are critical or ungrateful |
| _____ d. gossip (Prov. 16:28) | 4. betraying a confidence or discussing unflattering personal facts about a person |
| _____ e. worthless talk (Eph. 4:20) | 5. saying what springs to mind without thinking about consequences |
| _____ f. grumbling and complaining (Jas. 5:9) | 6. speaking false, malicious words about another person |

### (2) Controlling Others (2 Tim. 2:25)

### (3) Breaking Our Word (Ps. 15:4)

**(4) Failing to Respect Authority (Rom. 13:1-7)**

**(5) Forgetting the Golden Rule (Matt. 7:12)**

**(6) Serving Sinful Desires (1 John 2:15-17)**

**4. The Seven A's of Confession**
**Put a star by the "A" you consider the most difficult**
**to do in the act of confession.**

(1) Address everyone involved.
(2) Avoid "if", "but", and "maybe".
(3) Admit specifically.
(4) Acknowledge the hurt.
(5) Accept the consequences.
(6) Alter your behavior.
(7) Ask forgiveness; allow time.

**5. Write a prayer to God, asking Him to help you with**
**the "A" you starred in the "Seven A's of Confession"**
**above.**

_____
_____
_____
_____
_____
_____

**6. As you watch "I'm Really Sorry" from _Peacemaker_**
**_Parables_, answer these questions:**

   a. What was wrong with the husband's apology?

   _____
   _____

b. How did the wife contribute to the conflict?

_____

_____

**7. Read the following story, "A Fast Turnaround." Then answer the questions below it.**

### A Fast Turnaround

One sin that we frequently commit against others is to fail to overlook minor offenses (Prov. 19:11). One way to overcome this habit is to think deliberately about aspects of your opponent that are true, noble, right, pure, lovely, admirable, excellent, or praiseworthy (see Phil. 4:8).

One day Corlette said something that really hurt me. I didn't remember what she said, but I remember going out into the back yard to rake leaves. The more I dwelt on her words, the more deeply I slid into self-pity and resentment. Then God brought Philippians 4:8 to my mind.

"Nothing's noble, right, or lovely about the way she's treating me," I thought. But the Holy Spirit wouldn't give up. The verse would not go away. Finally, to get God off my back, I grudgingly conceded that Corlette is a good cook. This small concession opened the door to a stream of thoughts about my wife's good qualities. I recalled that she keeps a beautiful home and practices wonderful hospitality. She always has been kind toward my family and never missed a chance to share the gospel with my father (who eventually trusted Christ just two hours before he died.)

I realized that Corlette always has been pure and faithful. She has supported me through difficult times in my work. Every chance she gets, she attends the seminars I teach and sits smiling and supportive through the same material she has heard over and over. She has even taken up backpacking because she knows I love it!

Soon my attitude toward her turned upside down. I saw her offensive comment for exactly what it was worth—a momentary flaw in an otherwise wonderful person. I dropped my rake and went inside but not to unload a storm of resentment. To her surprise, I walked in, gave her a big hug, and told her how glad I was to be married to her. As I admitted that I had made a mountain out of a molehill, we moved quickly to a warm reconciliation.

**Answer these questions about what you just read:**
a. On a scale of 1 to 10, with 1 being "extremely difficult" and 10 being "extremely easy", how difficult would it be for you to take the same step that author Ken Sande did in his conflict with his wife, as described in the story you just read?

_____

b. Read Proverbs 11:27. What do you think this verse has to say about thinking whatever is noble, right, or lovely about someone who has offended you?

_____

c. Have you ever had a time when focusing on the positive aspects of your opponent helped speed reconciliation? If so, describe here.

_____

_____

**8. For further study:**
a. Read *The Peacemaker* (3d ed.) (pp. 117-135).
b. Complete "A Fast Turnaround" (pp. 42-43) if you did not do so in class.
c. Do the week-4 Daily Devotionals, adapted from *The Peacemaker* (pp. 44-48).
d. Complete "If You Are Presently Involved in a Conflict" (pp. 49-51).

# Day 1. Trouble on the Job

*Today's verse: Bear with each other and forgive whatever grievances you may have against one another. Forgive as the Lord forgave you (Col. 3:13).*

Ted worked for a government agency. As a new believer, he was excited about his salvation. Among his co-workers he wanted to have a positive witness for Christ.

However, he hit a snag when he tried to relate to Joan, his supervisor. Ted and Joan had never gotten along well, partly because Ted continually tried to tell her how to run her department. His newfound enthusiasm for Christ provoked her further.

As she became more and more annoyed with Ted, Joan gave him a particularly difficult work assignment that involved lifting things, even though she knew he had a back problem.

Eventually, he injured his back and had to leave work for several months. Although he received some disability benefits, Ted lost several thousand dollars in wages and medical expenses. As a result, he filed a lawsuit against Joan and the agency.

How might this latest challenge harm Ted's Christian witness? Ted didn't feel particularly good about filing the lawsuit, but he knew he and his family deserved some compensation for his injury.

*Lord, I so desperately want to be a good witness for you, yet I find that situations in the workplace and in the real world constantly threaten my Christian example. In every instance grant Your wisdom.*

# Day 2. Owning His Contribution

*Today's verse: Starting a quarrel is like breaching a dam; so drop the matter before a dispute breaks out (Prov. 17:14).*

By the time Ted visited me for some counsel on how to deal with his case, he had returned to work. The lawsuit was moving slowly through the court system.

During our first conversation, Ted and I identified several ways he had contributed to the conflict with Joan. Ted now was able to see his own fault more clearly. He began to consider settling the lawsuit by accepting the $5,000 the agency had offered him a few days earlier. Although his damages exceeded that amount, his attorney advised him to accept the settlement. On the other hand, several of Ted's friends encouraged him to demand more money or to continue the litigation.

A few days later Ted surprised me by saying that he planned to drop his lawsuit without accepting the settlement offer. The more he had reflected on his own fault in the matter, the less comfortable he felt about accepting money from the agency.

At the same time, he had concluded that laying down his right to restitution would be an effective way to demonstrate the mercy and forgiveness that he himself had received from God.

All that remained was for Ted to go talk with Joan. How would Joan respond to this surprising development?

*God, thank You for times that You help remove the blinders from my eyes so I can see my part in a dispute. Help me be alert to what You're trying to teach me.*

## Day 3. Doing the Right Thing

*Today's verse: Let your gentleness be evident to all. The Lord is near (Phil. 4:5).*

The next morning, Ted went to talk with Joan. He admitted that he had been disrespectful, arrogant, and rude. He asked for her forgiveness. Joan was surprised and seemed to suspect Ted's motives. In response she said little.

Ted went on to explain that he had forgiven her for ordering him to move the heavy boxes and that he was dropping his lawsuit. Finally he said he hoped they could start over in their relationship and learn to work together in the future.

More suspicious than ever, Joan asked why Ted was doing this. He replied, "I became a Christian a year ago. God is slowly helping me to face up to a lot of my faults, including those that contributed to the problems between you and me. God also has shown me that His love and forgiveness for me are absolutely free. I can do nothing to earn or deserve them. Since He has done that for me, I decided I wanted to act the same way toward you."

Joan, somewhat amazed by his answer, mumbled something like, "Oh, I see. Well, let's let bygones be bygones then. Thanks for stopping by."

Although Joan's response wasn't quite what Ted had hoped, he walked out of her office knowing that God had forgiven him and that he had at least given Joan a glimpse of that forgiveness.

*Lord, help me to remember that I may be the only Christian someone may know. Help me to always demonstrate Your love and forgiveness.*

# Day 4. Ripple Effect

*Today's verse: A man's wisdom gives him patience; it is to his glory to overlook an offense (Prov. 19:11).*

Ted soon discovered that Joan was telling others about their meeting. The next day a union representative who had heartily supported the lawsuit against Joan confronted Ted and asked whether he had really dropped his lawsuit.

When Ted said yes, the man asked, "Is it true that you did it because you're a Christian?" Ted again responded yes. The man's scowl turned to a look of puzzlement. As the man walked away, Ted heard him say to a bystander, "Well, that's the first time I've seen a Christian's faith cost him anything."

Like ripples in a pond, word of Ted's actions spread throughout the department. Any time someone asked Ted about the status of his pending lawsuit, Ted explained that he had dropped it and was not pursuing action against Joan and the department. It gave him a chance to explain the same thing he told Joan—that he was a Christian and wanted to model the way Christ responded to difficulty.

A few days later, two co-workers asked Ted to meet with them over lunch to discuss the Bible. Later, other co-workers asked Ted questions about his faith.

For the first time since Ted's conversion, he believed he was really helping people to learn about God's love.

*The world says one thing about how we resolve conflicts—with bitterness and strife—while You give another set of directions. O God, help us through our conflicts to demonstrate Christ's love.*

## Day 5. The Beam and the Mote

*Today's verse: Why do you look at the speck of sawdust in your brother's eye and pay no attention to the plank in your own eye? (Matt. 7:3).*

Although Joan at times continued to treat Ted rudely, he learned to submit to her authority and to use her provocations as further opportunities to show God's work in his life. When Joan was replaced a few months later, Ted had no doubt in his mind Who had arranged for him to have a more pleasant and supportive boss.

Three years later, I asked Ted whether he regretted his decision to give up the settlement. "No", he replied. "That was the best $5,000 I ever spent. God used those events to bring several people to Christ. He also helped me to overcome some major sins in my life. I only wish I had settled more quickly."

Many conflicts require much time and effort to resolve. But far more can be resolved simply by overlooking minor offenses or relinquishing rights for the sake of God's Kingdom. Sometimes we can grow by owning our part in the conflict and realizing that we are not an innocent party.

Therefore, before focusing on your rights, look carefully at your responsibilities. Before you go to remove the speck from your brother's eye, ask yourself, "Is this really worth fighting over?"

*Help me discern, dear Father, when battles truly are worth pursuing and when others are best dropped because I, too, have played a role.*

## If You Are Presently Involved in a Conflict

If you are presently involved in a conflict, these questions will help you to apply the principles presented in this chapter.

1. As you look back at the way you have dealt with this conflict, do you see a need for repentance and confession?

2. As you have talked to and about others in this situation, have you used your tongue as a weapon in any of the following kinds of speech? If so, describe what you said.
   - reckless words
   - grumbling and complaining
   - falsehood
   - gossip
   - slander
   - worthless talk that does not benefit or build others up

3. Have you tried to control others in this situation? Why and how?

4. Are you guilty of any of the following sins in this situation? If so, describe what you did or failed to do.
   - uncontrolled anger
   - bitterness
   - vengeance
   - evil or malicious thoughts
   - sexual immorality
   - substance abuse
   - laziness
   - defensiveness

- self-justification
- stubbornness
- resistance to godly advice
- greed
- deficient work
- withholding mercy and forgiveness
- improper concessions
- compulsive behavior
- breaking your word
- misusing authority
- rebelling against authority
- failing to treat others as you want to be treated

5. Have any of the following idols/desires influenced your behavior in this situation? How?
- lust of the flesh
- pride
- love of money
- fear of others (or excessive concern about what others think of you)
- good things you want too much (desires elevated to demands)

6. How have your sins contributed to this conflict?

7. Write an outline for your confession (use the blank space on p. 51).
   a. **Address** everyone involved.
   b. **Avoid** "if", "but", and "maybe." What excuses or blaming do you need to avoid?
   c. **Admit** specifically. What desires have you allowed to rule you, and what sins have you committed? What biblical principles have you violated?
   d. **Acknowledge** the hurt. How might others feel as a result of your sin?
   e. **Accept** the consequences. What consequences do you need to accept? How can you reverse the damage you have caused?

f. **Alter** your behavior. What changes do you need to
make, with God's help, in the way you think, speak,
or behave in the future?
g. **Ask** for forgiveness. What might make the person
whom you have wronged reluctant to forgive you?
What can you do to make forgiving you easier for
that person?


8. How do you want to change as a result of this conflict?
What one character quality do you wish to change?
Specifically, what steps can you take to practice that
quality?


9. Go on record with the Lord by writing a prayer based
on the principles this chapter teaches.

## *Week 5: Just Between the Two of You*

**1. Describe a time when you chose to overlook an offense.**

_____

_____

_____

Describe a time when you decided to approach someone about a wrong that person committed.

_____

_____

**2. Look up the verses to determine how each person used alternatives to direct confrontation to point out wrongdoing to others.**

   a. Jesus with the Samaritan woman (John 4:1-18)

     *questions & discussion*

   b. Jesus with the chief priests and elders
     (Matt. 21:33-45)

     *parables + stories*

   c. Paul with the Athenians (Acts 17:22-31)

     *point of common interest*

   d. Esther with the king (Esther 5:1-8; 7:1-4)

     *used banquets*

3. Have you ever used an intermediary or other concerned person to prepare the way before you approached someone about a problem? If so, describe below.

_____

_____

_____

4. Can you easily approach another person who has something against you, even if you believe you did nothing to contribute to the alienation? Why or why not?

_____

_____

5. What are the four criteria for determining whether another person's sin is so serious that talking with the person is advisable? Fill in the blanks below.

Is it dishonoring God?
Is it damaging your relationship?
Is it hurting others?
Is it hurting the offender?

6. Special Considerations
Below write answers to questions that might arise when one considers confronting in a situation that involves a special circumstance.

How might you approach a non-Christian?

_____

_____

How might you approach a person in authority over you?

_____

_____

How might you approach an abuser?

_____

_____

How might you deal with someone who has not responded well to your first approach?

_____

_____

### 7. After the Log Is Out of Your Eye

**What would you say/do if—**
a person follows your confession with a lukewarm or incomplete confession, such as: "I guess I sort of lost my temper, too"?

_____

_____

a person follows your confession by accepting your apology yet mentions nothing that he or she did wrong?

_____

_____

you decide, from your initial interaction, that the matter is not urgent and immediate confrontation is not likely to be productive?

_____

_____

### 8. As you watch "Slippery Slope Denial" from *Peacemaker Parables*, answer these questions:

a. What aspect of the Slippery Slope was Clare following?

_____

_____

b. What role did her daughter play?

_____

_____

**9. For further study:**

    a. Read *The Peacemaker* (3d ed.) (pp. 139-160). For additional insights in how to speak the truth in love, see pages 162-183.

    b. Complete "After the Log Is Out of Your Eye" (p. 54) if you did not do so in class.

    c. Do the week-5 Daily Devotionals, adapted from *The Peacemaker* (pp. 56-60).

    d. Complete "If You Are Presently Involved in a Conflict" (pp. 61-62).

# Day 1. The Talk after Class

*Today's verse: Brothers, if someone is caught in a sin, you who are spiritual should restore him gently (Gal. 6:1).*

Janet waited patiently for the last group of Larry's students to file out the door. When she saw that he was finished with his work and was placing papers into his briefcase, she walked casually into his classroom.

Giving him a friendly smile, she asked, "Larry, do you have a few minutes to talk?"

Larry looked up, his eyes filled with suspicion. "I'm pretty busy right now. What do you want to talk about?"

"I'd like to ask your forgiveness for the way I spoke to you last week. I'd like to talk about how we are relating to each other. If this isn't a convenient time, I could come back later."

His surprised look showed that this was not what he was expecting to hear from Janet. "No, that's okay. I've got a few minutes."

"Thanks. Well, like I said, I need to ask your forgiveness for what I said in the teachers lounge last Wednesday. When you joked about me in front of Steve and Joyce, I lost my temper and lashed back at you. I was wrong. I'm sure I embarrassed you. Would you please forgive me?"

Taken off-guard by her transparency, all Larry could think to say was, "That's okay. I know I can be sort of abrasive at times. Just forget about it."

That's exactly what Janet could have done at this point—just drop it. That would be that. But Janet was more concerned about her long-term relationship with Larry than about simply smoothing over this conflict. She said a prayer and pondered what she could say next.

*I make so many mistakes in relationships, Lord. Many times I speak before I think. Help me to turn to You for Your guidance in day-to-day conversations.*

# Day 2. Getting to the Heart of Things

*Today's verse: Better is open rebuke than hidden love. Wounds from a friend can be trusted, but an enemy multiplies kisses (Prov. 27:5-6).*

For days Janet had been planning her conversation. A trained reconciler in her church had helped her. In discussing various scenarios, they had anticipated that Larry might try to brush their differences aside, so they had role-played how to keep the conversation going. When Larry said to "forget it", Janet now put that planning into practice.

"Since I blew up at you in front of Steve and Joyce, I want you to know that I plan to go to them and admit my wrong. Can I do anything else to make this right with you? Have I done anything else to offend you?"

"No", he responded, "not that I can think of."

"Maybe you can help me understand something. If I haven't done anything else to offend you, why do you say sarcastic things about me in front of others?"

"Hey, I'm just kidding around. Can't you take a joke?"

"Maybe you don't mean to hurt me, but it doesn't feel like a joke, Larry. I feel embarrassed when I'm made fun of in front of people. And I don't think I'm the only person who's staying clear of the teachers lounge just to avoid your jokes."

"Oh, so now I'm the big bad wolf," Larry responded snidely. "All the little pigs need to run home to hide."

"That's just what I mean, Larry. You seem to have a habit of calling people names and tearing them down. It's not a good example for our students."

Janet knew that if she wanted to gently restore Larry, she couldn't back down now. But Larry was becoming more and more defensive. His face was getting red. She had to decide whether to go on with the next scenario she and her reconciler had outlined.

*Lord, help me take seriously Your command that we help restore others. Help me to have courage when the conversation threatens to become unpleasant.*

## Day 3. What Kind of Witness?

*Today's verse: And the Lord's servant must not quarrel; instead, he must be kind to everyone, able to teach, not resentful. Those who oppose him he must gently instruct, in the hope that God will grant them repentance leading them to knowledge of the truth (2 Tim. 2:24-25).*

Janet took a deep breath and continued to talk to Larry.

"You know, Larry, I'm sorry to have to say this, but I've overheard some of the staff mocking you to your back. Do you know what they're saying?"

Larry didn't actually want to know, but he felt compelled to reply, "What?"

"They're calling you a hypocrite, Larry. They can't understand how you can claim to be a Christian and speak so critically all the time."

Larry cringed at Janet's words. He began looking for a way to end the conversation. Before he could reply, however, Janet spoke gently.

"I don't think you mean to do it. I believe you want to have a positive witness, but you seem to be stuck in the habit of saying hurtful things to people. I've struggled with the same problem, Larry. I've hurt so many people with my words. Just ask my family! But God is so forgiving. He doesn't treat us as our sins deserve. And He wants to free us from our hurtful habits. He doesn't want you and me fighting with each other. He would be so pleased if we forgave each other and worked together to improve our relationship and our witness around here."

Janet had done it. She had spoken the words that God put on her heart. She hadn't yelled or accused. She had simply laid out on the table how she felt and her concerns about the relationship. The rest was up to Larry.

*I pray you'll help me, God, to be aware of how my bickering and backbiting with people harms how others see You. Help me to make positive changes.*

# Day 4. A Glimmer of Hope

*Today's verse: Do nothing out of selfish ambition or vain conceit, but in humility consider others better than yourselves. Each of you should look not only to your own interests, but also to the interests of others (Phil 2:3-4).*

Larry had never been approached in the manner Janet had just addressed him. Usually people fired back at him in anger or gave him a strong dose of his own sarcastic humor. Or they stopped having anything to do with him altogether, like Janet had described. Of course, when they began snubbing him, Larry had rationalized that they were just weak or wimpish or too serious for their own good.

The truth in Janet's words stung, but her tone of voice, which had remained calm and unruffled, and her reminder of God's forgiveness held out a glimmer of hope. He slumped in his chair and sighed with weariness and regret.

"I don't deserve your forgiveness," Larry told Janet. "I've torn you apart all year, just like I have everyone else. I've always used sarcasm when I don't know how to relate to people. Night after night I go home knowing I blew it, but I can't seem to change. Do you think any hope really exists for a jerk like me?"

"Of course!" Janet replied as she pulled up a chair across from Larry's desk. "If God can help me get control of my tongue, He can help anyone. Let's pray right now and ask Him to show us how we can turn our past differences into an opportunity to demonstrate His power in our lives."

*Thank You, precious Jesus, that through You, I can find hope for dealing with all relationships.*

## Day 5. A Whole New Approach

*Today's verse: My brothers, if one of you should wander from the truth and someone should bring him back, remember this: Whoever turns a sinner from the error of his way will save him from death and cover over a multitude of sins (Jas. 5:19-20).*

Talking to other people about a conflict usually is an unpleasant experience. We often let tensions build to the exploding point and then confront people with a list of their wrongs. They become defensive and react with a list of our shortcomings, which leads to a painful battle of words. Those who are more verbally skilled may win a few arguments this way, but in the process, they lose many important relationships.

The gospel opens the door for an entirely different approach to talking to others about their role in a conflict. Remembering God's mercy toward us, we can approach others in a spirit of love rather than condemnation.

Instead of using guilt and shame to force others to change themselves, we can breathe grace by holding out to them the wonderful news that God wants to free them from sin and help them grow to be like His Son.

We can learn many helpful communications skills. These enable us to listen more carefully and speak more clearly and graciously. Godly communication usually leads to better understanding and agreement.

As your words are seasoned with wisdom and grace, talking to others about their wrongs can become an avenue for strengthening relationships, serving other people, and bringing praise to God.

*Lord, I'm willing to try a new tactic in how I relate to others, but I can only do this with Your help. Thank You that You are always with me.*

### If You Are Presently Involved in a Conflict

If you are presently involved in a conflict, these questions will help you apply the principles from this week's lesson.

1. Do you have any reason to believe that someone has something against you? If so, why?

2. How has the other person sinned in this situation?

3. Would overlooking the offense against you be better, or should you go and talk with the other person? What would be the probable benefits and drawbacks of each course of action?

4. Is the other person's sin too serious to overlook? More specifically, does it dishonor God? If so, how?

Is it damaging your relationship? If so, how?

Is it hurting others? If so, how?

Is it hurting that person? If so, how?

Is it making that person less useful to the Lord? If so, how?

5. Which of the other person's sins need to be discussed?

6. Would going in person be better, or would involving others right away be best? Why?

7. Would raising the issue directly be best, or might this person respond better to an indirect approach? How could you use a story, an analogy, or a point of common interest to open your discussion?

8. Do you need to confess any of your sins before you talk about what the other person has done wrong? If so, what will you do if the other person does not confess his or her sins?

9. Go on record with the Lord by writing a prayer based on the principles taught in this session.

## *Week 6: Forgive As God Forgave You*

1. Think of a time that you have prayed a prayer similar to the one Ken Sande prayed in the opening illustration. If you have ever prayed such a prayer—asking God to help you forgive in His strength and not in yours—describe that situation below.

_____

_____

_____

2. Below are listed the three statements about what forgiveness is not. Put a star by which of the three, if any, is the most surprising to you.

- Forgiveness is not a feeling.
✶• Forgiveness is not forgetting.
- Forgiveness is not excusing.

3. Describe a time you have extracted a payment from a person who sinned against you.

_____

_____

_____

What were the short-term consequences? the long-term consequences?

_____

_____

4. Describe a time when God had deposited in your account more than an ample amount of grace that you needed to make the payments of forgiveness for someone who wronged you.

_____

_____

_____


5. Put a star by the promise you believe is the most difficult to make in the area of forgiveness.

- I will not dwell on this incident.
- I will not bring up this incident again and use it against you.
- I will not talk to others about this incident.
- I will not let this incident stand between us or hinder our personal relationship.

6. Write a prayer, asking God to help you in the area you starred in item 5.

_____

_____

_____

_____

_____


7. Describe your response to this statement in lesson 6: "Forgiveness provides an excellent opportunity to glorify God by sharing what Jesus did on the cross and how His love is the model for your forgiveness." How do you feel when you read this statement?

_____

_____

_____


Have you ever done this before—used the occasion of your forgiveness of someone as an opportunity to share about Jesus? If so, what was the outcome?

_____

_____

**8. Fill in the blank words missing in these two steps to forgiveness.**

The first step, having an _____ of forgiveness, is unconditional and is a commitment you make to God (see Mark 11:25).
The second step, _____ forgiveness, is conditional on the offender's repentance and occurs between you and that person (see Luke 17:3-5).

**9. Put a check mark beside the situation(s) in which the most loving approach may well be to not release the person from the consequences of his or her sin/action.**

____ a treasurer who secretly stole from your church

____ a teen-ager who drove carelessly in your neighborhood and knocked over your curbside mailbox

____ an employee who, because of family pressures, neglected work responsibilities and is in danger of losing his or her job

____ a friend who accidentally dropped and broke a coffee cup from your fine-china set while she visited you

**10. After watching "Forgive You?" from the *Peacemaker Parables*, answer these questions:**

How well do you think Rick did in apologizing to Andy?
_____
_____

How would you evaluate Andy's response in terms of the four promises that are essential elements of forgiveness?
_____
_____
_____

**11. For further study:**
   a. Read *The Peacemaker* (3d ed.) (pp. 201-213).
   b. Do the week-6 Daily Devotionals, adapted from *The Peacemaker* (pp. 67-71).
   c. Complete, "If You Are Presently Involved in a Conflict" (pp. 72-73).

**Devotional Readings for Week 6**

# Day 1. "I Can't Be Close Again."

*Today's verse: Forgive us our debts, as we also have forgiven our debtors (Matt. 6:12).*

"I just can't forgive Pam's adultery," Rick said. "She says she's sorry; she's begged for forgiveness. But I can't forget what she did. It's like a huge wall between us; I can't get through it."

"So you think divorce is the answer?" I asked.

"I don't know what else to do! I told her that I forgive her, but I just can't be close to her again. She's depressed and has withdrawn even further from me. I'm afraid she's going to look for intimacy with someone else again. We're both in agony. I wonder whether we'd be better off divorced."

I could see the weariness in his face. "I'm sure both of you are in terrible pain, Rick. But I don't think divorce will end it. You'll just trade one kind of pain for another."

Rick looked thoughtful and receptive. I wondered how he would react if I made the proposal to him that I had in mind.

*Help me turn to You, Father, when all visible means of hope are gone. Keep me open to your answers.*

## Day 2. Empty Forgiveness

*Today's verse: I will forgive their wickedness and will remember their sins no more (Jer. 31:34b).*

"Rick, imagine that you had just confessed a serious sin to God," I said. "Then, for the first time in your life, He spoke to you audibly. He said, 'I forgive you, Rick, but I can't ever be close to you again.' How would you feel?"

After an awkward pause, he replied, "I guess I'd feel as though God hadn't really forgiven me."

"But isn't that exactly the way you are forgiving Pam?" I asked.

Rick looked at the floor, wrestling for an answer.

In a softer voice, I continued, "Imagine that God said, 'Rick, I forgive you. I promise never to think about your sin again or to dwell on it or brood over it. I promise never to bring it up and use it against you. I promise not to talk to others about it. And I promise not to let this sin stand between us or to hinder our relationship.'"

After a long silence, tears began to fill Rick's eyes. "I would know I was completely forgiven. But I wouldn't deserve that kind of forgiveness after the way I've treated Pam."

*Thank You for your reminder, Lord, that Your gracious treatment of us is the model for the way in which we are to treat others.*

# Day 3. Forgiveness—a Choice

*Today's verse: Bear with each other and forgive whatever grievances you may have against one another. Forgive as the Lord forgave you (Col. 3:13).*

Rick's last statement was correct about one thing. He didn't deserve God's forgiveness after the way he treated Pam.

"Would you ever deserve it?" I asked. "God's forgiveness is a free gift, purchased for you by Jesus' death on the cross. He doesn't forgive you because you've earned it. He forgives you because He loves you. When you truly understand how precious and undeserved His forgiveness is, you will want to forgive Pam in the same way He has forgiven you."

"I know I should, but how could I ever keep those promises? I can't imagine forgetting what Pam did! And I just don't feel as though I can ever be close to her again."

"Hold on, Rick. Where in the Bible do you find that forgiveness means forgetting? Or that it depends on feelings? Forgiveness is a choice—a decision you make by God's grace in spite of your feelings. Of course forgiving is difficult, especially in a case like this. But if you ask for God's help as you make those promises to Pam, He will give you the grace to follow through on them."

*You help us to do the impossible, Lord. Thank You that You are the wind beneath our wings in difficult situations.*

## Day 4. Turning Point

*Today's verse: First go and be reconciled to your brother; then come and offer your gift (Matt. 5:24b).*

Rick and I talked another 30 minutes about God's forgiveness. As Rick reflected on how much God had forgiven him, he discovered a longing to do the same with Pam.

We prayed together. Then I called Pam and asked her to join us at my office. When she arrived, doubt and fear were written all over her face. She appeared to be very troubled about why I had called her.

She quickly discovered why. As soon as she sat down, Rick began, "Pam, I need to ask for your forgiveness. I have sinned so terribly against you. You asked me to forgive you, but I wouldn't give you real forgiveness. Instead, I have punished you with my bitterness and coldness. I have been so wrong. Will you please forgive me?"

Pam dissolved in tears. In between sobs, she poured out her own feelings of guilt and shame, along with her fear that Rick could never really forget what she had done.

Reaching out to take her hand, Rick responded, "I can understand your fear. I haven't dealt with this the way I should have. I forgot how much God has forgiven me. But he has helped me today. I want to forgive you the way He has forgiven me."

What do you think will happen to Rick and Pam as a result of what Rick just said and did while he sat in my office?

*Your forgiveness of me is unfathomable, Lord. You do not treat me as my sins deserve. Help me extend that forgiveness to others.*

# Day 5. Clearing a Path

*Today's verse: As far as the east is from the west, so far has he removed our transgressions from us (Ps. 103:12).*

After both Rick and Pam confessed their sins to each other, Rick wrapped his arms around Pam. They cried together for several minutes. By offering her the redeeming forgiveness our Lord modeled, Rick had brought life and hope back into their marriage.

Although they would need to spend many more hours of pastoral counseling to address the root causes of their marital problems, forgiveness had cleared a path through the rubble of the past.

By God's grace, Rick and Pam could now deal with those problems in a way that could result in a completely restored marriage and a powerful testimony to the reconciling power of Jesus Christ.

In working with Rick and Pam, I was reminded of the way in which I have learned to respond when I need to forgive my children for something they have done.

I pull them onto my lap, put my arms around them, and remind them of the forgiveness we all have in Christ, which enables me to forgive them. Then I recite Corlette's poem to them, "Good thought, Hurt you not, Gossip never, Friends forever." As I say "Friends forever" softly in their ears, I hug them close. I want them to know that no matter what they have done wrong, Jesus has opened the way for a complete restoration of our relationship. I hope that as they experience genuine, affectionate reconciliation with me over and over again, they will eventually know more fully the far-better forgiveness they will always find when they run into the arms of God through prayer and faith.

*Help me model what You would do in every situation, Lord, because I know that I may be the only representative of You that others see.*

## If You Are Presently Involved in a Conflict

Answering these questions will help you apply to your situation the principles presented in this week's study.

1. How has your opponent sinned against you?

2. Which of these sins has your opponent confessed?

3. Which of the unconfessed sins can you overlook and forgive at this time?

4. Take the first step of forgiveness: admit that you cannot forgive on your own. Ask God to change your heart.

5. Now write out the four promises that you will make to your opponent at this time to indicate your forgiveness.

6. What consequences of your opponent's sin will you take on yourself? What consequences will you expect your opponent to bear?

7. If you are having a difficult time forgiving your opponent:
   a. Is this because you are not sure he or she has repented? If so, how could you encourage confirmation of repentance?
   b. Do you think your opponent must somehow earn or deserve your forgiveness? Are you trying to punish by

withholding forgiveness? Are you expecting a guarantee that the offense will not happen again? If you have any of these attitudes or expectations, what do you need to do?

c. How did your sins contribute to this problem? Which of these sins will God refuse to forgive if you repent? How can you imitate His forgiveness?

d. Read Matthew 18:21-35. What is the point of this passage? How does it apply to you? How might God be working for good in your situation?

e. For what has God forgiven you in the past? How serious are your opponent's sins against you when compared with your sins against God? How can you show God that you appreciate His forgiveness?

8. How can you demonstrate forgiveness or promote reconciliation

a. in thought?

b. in word?

c. in deed?

9. Go on record with the Lord by writing a prayer based on the principles this chapter teaches.

# Second Six Weeks

*Week 1: Speak the Truth in Love*

**1. In the following passages, describe how the speaker or writer set a positive context for correction.**

Jesus with the Samaritan woman (John 4:7-26)

_____

_____

_____

Jesus with the hard-hearted Pharisees (Luke 19:1-10)

_____

_____

_____

Paul with the erring Corinthians (1 Cor. 1:2-9)

_____

_____

_____

Paul in admonishing the Colossians (Col. 1:3-23)

_____

_____

_____

**2. Match the listening skill in the left-hand column with the correct example of that skill in the right-hand column. Put a star beside the skill that is the easiest for you to do and a check mark by the one most difficult for you.**

_____ 1. waiting     a. "Can you give me an example?"

_____ 2. attending    b. "I see." "Uh-huh."

_____ 3. clarifying    c. "You seem to believe I was being dishonest about . . .."

_____ 4. reflecting    d. "A lot of what you said is true."

_____ 5. agreeing    e. Being comfortable with silence

**3. Think about a time in which you used one of the communications skills just described (breathe grace, make charitable judgments, speak the truth in love, help others examine the desires of their hearts, choose the right time and place) in an effort to resolve a conflict. Below, write about that time.**

_____

_____

_____

**4. The case studies that follow are examples of which communications skill you just heard about? (Possible answers: engaging rather than declaring; planning your words; talking from beside, not from above; talking in ing "I" statements)**

_____ 1. Kevin's first reaction when he realized that his boss filled the section manager job without notifying him was to storm into his boss' office and say, "You made the appointment without even consulting me. How could you do that to me?" Then Kevin stopped himself and asked himself the question, "What do I really

feel about this situation? What about it makes me angry?"
He then realized he needed to approach his boss in this
manner: "I feel embarrassed because everyone in the section knew about the section manager appointment before
I did."

_____ 2. Clare wanted her brother, Brian,
to know how hurt she felt when he missed her birthday
this year—for the second year in a row! She typed an
angry, lengthy email to him and was about to send it to
him at his office. Then she paused and decided instead to
call Brian to make an appointment to meet with him over
coffee.

_____ 3. Carter was furious because Mom
had called his home, demanding to know why he and his
wife wouldn't be spending Christmas with her and Dad
again this year. He wanted to rush over to her house and
tell her to stay out of their business, but he knew Mom
would be angry and defensive if he just blurted out what
he was thinking. He didn't want to rupture his relationship with his mother, yet he wasn't sure how to help her
understand about her meddling. Then he thought about
Mom's passion for gardening. Perhaps he could talk
about how he and his wife need space to grow in much
the same way that Mom's jonquil bulbs need to be plant-
ed a certain distance apart so they have adequate growing
space.

**5. What skill just mentioned (use the Bible carefully, ask
for feedback, offer solutions and preferences, recognize
your limits, be objective) does the speaker in each example fail to use or use improperly?**

_____ 1. "You never remember to take the trash
out on garbage day."
_____ 2. "I used an 'I' statement when I talked to
Tom. Why did he still refuse to apologize?"
_____ 3. "The Bible says to love your neighbor as
yourself. Therefore, you need to make sure
your dog never strays over to my lawn."

**6. After watching "Word Pictures" from *Peacemaker Parables,* answer these questions:**

How successful was Janet in using word pictures to describe her feelings about her marriage to Jim? Would some other approach have been more effective?

_____

_____


Which of the communications skills you have learned in this week-1 study did Janet and Jim fail to use in working out their conflict?

_____

_____

_____


**Fill in the blanks:**
Years and years of peace-_____ exploded in a fit of peace-_____ but were finally resolved through genuine peace-_____.

What skills could have kept the issues between Jim and Janet resolved on a day-to-day basis instead of allowing them to build up over a five-year period?

_____

_____

_____


**7. For further study:**
  a. Read *The Peacemaker* (3d ed.) (pp. 162-183).
  b. Do the week-1 Daily Devotionals, adapted from *The Peacemaker* (pp. 81-85).
  c. Complete "If You Are Presently Involved in a Conflict" (pp. 86-87).

## Devotional Readings for Week 1

# Day 1. Careful Planning

*Today's verse: Those who plan what is good find love and faithfulness (Prov. 14:22b).*

"Jim, this is Dave. I'm really sorry for what I said last Friday. I was wrong to cut you off. If you have some time in the next day or two, I'd like to stop by so I can apologize in person and see how you would like to finish this project. Would that be alright with you?"

Choosing your words carefully when you need to talk with others about their faults is critically important. Careful planning can make the difference between restored peace or increased hostility. Scripture highly commends the discipline of planning (see today's verse).

When you deal with important issues or sensitive people, think in advance about what you will say—even write it out. Define the problem as narrowly as possible, so you can focus on the central issues and not let minor details distract you. Avoid offensive words and topics, if at all possible. Although you can't write a script for your entire conversation, planning some of your opening comments can help a conversation begin positively. Try to use words that are gracious, clear, and constructive.

An opening statement such as the one in the first paragraph indicates that you don't want to continue an argument but rather to seek positive dialogue. Asking for a meeting is less threatening than is telling someone a meeting will be held.

Once the other person gives you an opportunity to talk, in person you can say, "Thank you for taking time to talk with me. Lately I've had the feeling that you are disappointed with my work. If I have done something wrong or if you know specific ways I can improve my work, I would really like to hear about them."

*Lord, help the words I choose to be Your words and not those that would do ill.*

## Day 2. When Tempers Flare

*Today's verse: A gentle answer turns aside wrath, but a harsh word stirs up anger (Prov. 15:1).*

Besides planning your opening remarks, like you read about in day 1, you are wise to think of two or three ways the other person may respond to your words. Plan how you will deal with each scenario. Even if the other person says something you had not anticipated, your preparation generally will make responding easier.

For example, you may anticipate that the person to whom you will speak may lose his or her temper. Here is a possible response:

"Ted, I can understand how frustrated you must be to have so much financial pressure. I also can see why you are upset about having to make a repair so soon after I sold the car to you. I'm trying to figure out what I should do about it. Knowing a little more about what went wrong with the engine would help. However, I think we could understand each other better if we talked in person. Could I stop by some evening this week?"

In responding to an angry reaction, remember the words of Proverbs 15:1 (above). In every way communicate that you take the other's expression of anger seriously and that you want to help resolve the problems that prompted it. Plan ahead how to respond to possible objections and deal with them specifically and reasonably.

If you believe that the other person may refuse to meet with you, you may plan this kind of response:

"Ted, I need to tell you that according to our contract, I do have the legal right to take the car back, keep your deposit, and let you worry about paying the repair bill. I'd rather not do that. I still would like to work this out in a way that is satisfactory to both of us. Would you at least be willing to think about what I'm suggesting? I'll call you back in a couple of days."

*Give me the strength, Lord, to respond gently to others' anger.*

# Day 3. A Mark of Spiritual Maturity

*Today's verse: Let a righteous man strike me—it is a kindness; let him rebuke me—it is oil on my head. My head will not refuse it (Ps. 141:5).*

Agreeing with what another person says is an especially powerful listening response in peacemaking. This doesn't mean you abandon your beliefs but rather that you acknowledge what you know is true before you address points of disagreement. Agreeing with the person who speaks often encourages him or her to talk more openly and avoid necessary repetition.

Agreeing is especially important when you have been in the wrong. Responses like these can make the difference between an argument and a meaningful dialogue:

"You're right. I was wrong when I said . . ."

"You know, a lot of what you just said is true. I do need to deal with my attitude."

When you talk with another person, first listen for the truth. Resist the temptation to defend yourself, blame others, or focus on points of disagreement. Acknowledge what is true in what the person says; identify your common ground before you move on to your differences. Doing so is a sign of wisdom and spiritual maturity.

One reason we sometimes hesitate to admit being wrong on one issue is that we fear we will seem as though we are accepting responsibility for the entire problem. The best way to overcome this hurdle is to agree with others in specific terms. Consider this example:

"Now that I've heard you, I can see that part of this problem really is my fault. I was wrong not to fulfill my part of the agreement. Then I made things even worse when I complained about you to others. What else do you believe I did wrong?" If you are humble enough to acknowledge where you were wrong, others are much more likely to do the same.

*Lord, help me to be mature enough to admit my faults.*

## Day 4. The Greatest Resource

*Today's verse: Do not let any unwholesome talk come out of your mouths, but only what is helpful for building others up according to their needs (Eph. 4:29).*

The Bible is our source of objective truth when we disagree with another Christian. If you don't use the Word with great care, however, it will alienate people rather than persuade them. You will sound "preachy" and "holier than thou"; the other person will believe you are talking down to him or her.

When you use the Scriptures as part of a discussion, keep Ephesians 4:29 in mind. Only use the Bible to build others up, not to tear them down. Make sure you are using a passage for its intended purpose. Don't pull a verse out of context and try to make it say something other than its clear meaning. If possible, encourage others to read the passage from their own Bibles; then ask, "What do you think that means?" This often achieves better results than does imposing your interpretation on them.

Know when to stop. If the other person appears to be growing annoyed with your references to Scripture, you may need to back off and let what you've said settle in. Backing off, however, is not appropriate if formal church discipline is under way and the person is clearly trying to avoid clear biblical warnings and admonishments.

An example would be, "Fred, I agree with you. This difference we're having about whether to battle Mrs. Jones over selling her land to a developer instead of the church, as she promised, is a major one. Lately, in my life, when someone has clearly wronged me, I've been turning to a passage in 2 Chronicles 20 about how to deal with my enemies. Would you consider reading this tonight in your own Bible at home? We could discuss it tomorrow as we plan our next step of action."

*Your Word is perfect, O God. Help me to remember its precepts when I feel stuck and believe no answer is to be found.*

# Day 5. Did I Say What I Think I Said?

*Today's verse: Speaking the truth in love, we will in all things grow up into him who is the Head, that is, Christ (Eph. 4:15).*

How can you know that you have been heard? One of your primary goals in problem-solving is to match impact with intent. Has the other person completely and accurately understood what you meant to say?

If the other person responds by clarifying, reflecting on, or agreeing with what you say, you will have a fairly good idea whether he or she has gotten your message.

In many cases, telling what impact your words are having on the other person will be difficult. Therefore, you will sometimes need to ask the other person to give you some feedback. Here are some ways you can do so:

"I'm not sure I've said this clearly. Would you mind telling me what you think I've said?"

"Have I confused you?"

"Have I explained myself clearly enough?"

"I've said what I think about the meeting. Tell me what your impressions are."

"What have I said that you would agree with? What would you disagree with?"

Asking questions will promote dialogue and will give you a sort of measuring stick about how well you are communicating as well as how the other person is responding to you. As you take that information into account, you can clarify as needed and adjust what you say according to how the conversation is developing. As a result, what you have left to say normally will be more relevant and productive.

As you practice these skills and make them a normal part of your everyday conversations, you will be well-prepared to use them when conflict breaks out. In developing the skills of loving confrontation, you can see for yourself that the "tongue of the wise brings healing."

*My greatest desire, Lord, is to be understood. Help me make myself clear in conversation so no misunderstandings occur.*

## If You Are Presently Involved in a Conflict

Answering these questions will help you apply to your situation the principles presented in this week's study.

1. When you talk to or about your opponent, what might you be tempted to say that would be harmful or worthless?

2. How can you offer hope to the other person by focusing on what God has done and is doing?

3. In this conflict, which listening skills do you have a difficult time with: waiting, attending, clarifying, reflecting, or agreeing? Write down some things you will do or say to overcome these weaknesses.

4. Are you trying to believe the best about the other person (i.e., making charitable judgments)? How can you demonstrate that you are doing this?

5. What can you say that would clearly communicate your love and concern for your opponent?

6. What is the best time and place to talk with your opponent?

7. Would you be wiser to communicate in person, on the phone, or by means of a letter? Why?

8. Write a brief summary of what you need to say and avoid saying. In your summary include

- issues that you believe should be addressed;

- words and topics to avoid;

- stories or comparisons that the other person will understand and value;

- words that describe your feelings;

- a description of the effect the dispute is having on you and others;

- your suggestions and preferences for a solution;

- the benefits that will be produced by cooperating to find a solution.

9. How could you improve what you intend to communicate so that you cannot be misunderstood?

10. Plan your opening statement. What are three ways that your opponent may react to this statement? How could you respond constructively to each of these reactions?

11. Write some of the "I" statements you could use.

12. How can you show that you are trying to be objective?

13. How can you refer to Scripture in a helpful manner?

14. How will you ask for feedback?

15. Go on record with the Lord by writing a prayer based on the principles this chapter teaches.

## *Week 2: Take One Or Two Others Along*

1. Write down the name or initials of a godly, wise person in the church who you would trust to help you resolve a conflict.

_____

2. Read Matthew 18:12-15 and 18:21-22. What is the main purpose of the process Jesus sets forth in verses 15-20?

_____
_____

3. In your Bible, look up the following Scriptures. What traits of a reconciler do these verses seem to indicate?

1 Corinthians 6:5 _____

Galatians 6:1 _____

4. Write down what types of tasks you think a reconciler might perform when called on to serve in a conflict situation.

_____
_____
_____

5. Read Acts 4:18-20 and 5:27-32. According to these passages, when may a Christian properly disobey his or her church when a church has made a final decision in a reconciliation situation?

_____

_____

6. Write some of your thoughts about step 5, "Treat Him as a Nonbeliever."

_____

_____

_____

7. Watch "Virtual Confrontation" from *Peacemaker Parables*. What is the main point of the parable?

_____

_____

8. Summarize the five steps Jesus commands us to take in Matthew 18:15-20 to restore a brother or sister who is caught in sin or conflict.

(1) _____ minor offenses.
(2) Talk in _____.
(3) Take one or two _____ along.
(4) Tell it to the _____.
(5) _____ him as a nonbeliever.

9. For further study:
   a. Read *The Peacemaker* (3d ed.) (pp. 185-199).
   b. Do the week-2 Daily Devotionals, adapted from *The Peacemaker* (pp. 90-94).
   c. Complete "If You Are Presently Involved in a Conflict" (p. 95).

# Day 1. A Marriage in Crisis

*Today's verse: What do you think? If a man owns a hundred sheep, and one of them wanders away, will he not leave the ninety-nine on the hills and go to look for the one that wandered off? (Matt. 18:12).*

Jim told Jennifer that he was filing for divorce to end their 25-year marriage. He said he was moving in with another woman. Jennifer tearfully and urgently begged Jim to reconsider, but he was adamant. Jennifer then went to their pastor for counsel.

Pastor Meadows gave her several suggestions on how to persuade Jim to change his mind or to at least consider visiting Pastor Meadows for counseling. However, nothing Jennifer said to her husband during the next few days dissuaded him. He began to pack his belongings.

In desperation, Jennifer returned to her pastor and asked him to talk with her husband.

At first Pastor Meadows declined to take an active role. He was concerned that in talking with Jim, he would "scare him away from the church."

However, Jennifer had done her homework and had read the Bible thoroughly. She asked Pastor Meadows how he could step aside from the conflict in light of Matthew 18:12-20, Galatians 6:1-2, and related passages.

Pastor Meadows took some time to study the passages that Jennifer had mentioned. After much study and more discussion with Jennifer, the pastor finally realized that he was neglecting his responsibility as a shepherd.

How would Pastor Meadows deal with this delicate issue in a way that communicated the seriousness of the situation to Jim yet still enabled him to come across as a loving, compassionate pastor?

*Lord, Your Word is true and is our ultimate authority. Help us to obey it in all of life's challenges.*

## Day 2. Get-Serious Time

*Today's verse: Brothers, if someone is caught in a sin, you who are spiritual should restore him gently. But watch yourself, or you also may be tempted. Carry each other's burdens, and in this way, you will fulfill the law of Christ (Gal. 6:1-2).*

In thinking more about how he would approach Jim, Pastor Meadows considered this analogy: When a patient has cancer, his doctor certainly would find telling the person difficult. Even so, any doctor who diagnoses cancer but who fails to report it to a patient would be guilty of malpractice. After all, a patient can be properly treated only after the disease has been identified.

Sin works in the same way. Left undiagnosed and untreated, it causes increasing grief and spiritual deterioration. The church has a responsibility both to promote peace and unity and to help believers disentangle themselves from the terrible effects of sin.

Treating someone as an unbeliever is a serious and painful step, but it is also an act of obedience to God and a loving remedy for the person caught in sin.

Pastor Meadows immediately went to Jim and offered to help him work out his marital problems. When Jim refused to change his course, the pastor pleaded with him to change his mind and offered all the church's resources to help solve the problems in his marriage.

When even that did not dissuade Jim, Pastor Meadows finally explained the Matthew 18 process and said, "I can't stop you from filing for divorce, but I must tell you that you may be removed from church membership if you deliberately violate Scripture as you are planning to do."

Jim's jaw dropped in surprise. Had he really heard correctly? Could the pastor really remove him from the church as he stated?

*Our sins are serious matters in Your eyes. We sometimes need to be reminded of this—and sometimes we also need to remind others. Help us always obey Your instruction.*

## Day 3. A Marriage Saved

*Today's verse: My son, do not despise the Lord's discipline and do not resent his rebuke, because the Lord disciplines those he loves, as a father the son he delights in (Prov. 3:11-12).*

After Jim got over his initial shock of the pastor's announcement—telling him his church membership would be revoked if he did not address his marital problems—Jim stormed, "You mean I'll be kicked out of the church for divorcing my wife?"

"Under these circumstances," the pastor replied, "yes." Hearing this, Jim lost his temper and ordered Pastor Meadows out of his home.

Early the next morning, however, Pastor Meadows answered his phone. Jim had called him, wanting to talk with the pastor again.

They met an hour later. By 10 a.m., Jim was on the telephone with the "other woman", telling her that he would not be moving in with her. He told her that their relationship was over and that he would be attempting to work things out with his wife.

Later that day, the pastor began counseling with Jim and Jennifer. Together they started to work out the serious problems that had brought them to this crisis.

Ten years later, they are still rearing their family together and thanking God for a pastor who cared enough to get involved the way Jesus commanded.

*The world thinks that confronting others about their sin is judgmental. Help me to believe your teaching that thoughtful correction actually is a sign of great love.*

# Day 4. Restoring Wandering Sheep

*Today's verse: He who heeds discipline shows the way to life, but whoever ignores correction leads others astray (Prov. 10:17).*

I wish I could say that all interventions turn out as well as the one did with Jim. Even so, I know of many marriages that are together today because churches obeyed Jesus' teaching in Matthew 18:15-20.

More importantly, even in those cases in which one party proceeded in a sinful course in spite of efforts to hold him or her accountable, the churches at least knew that they had been faithful to the Lord. Such faithfulness can significantly increase the respect that church members have for their leaders and for Scripture.

At the same time it sends a message that willful sin will not be casually overlooked. This encourages others in the church to work out their problems in a biblically faithful manner.

God views accountability and discipline as an act of love and as an important means to restore His wandering sheep and protect His people from being led astray by sinful examples.

By ignoring this teaching, a church not only disobeys Jesus' specific commands but also fails to face up to the seriousness of sin and its consequences.

This treatment is designed not to harm others but to bring conviction to stubborn people, with the purpose of leading them to turn from their sinful ways and to be restored to fellowship with God and fellow believers.

*Help me to remember, Lord, the responsibility I have in being accountable to you and my church and in helping hold others accountable as well.*

## Day 5. Preventing a Bad Example

*Today's verse: You who brag about the law, do you dishonor God by breaking the law? As it is written: "God's name is blasphemed among the Gentiles because of you" (Rom. 2:23-24).*

Treating someone as a nonbeliever serves three important purposes. First, revoking the person's membership in the church prevents the Lord from being dishonored if that person continues to act in blatantly sinful ways.

Second, other believers are protected from being led astray by a bad example. Romans 16:17 says, "I urge you, brothers, to watch out for those who cause divisions and put obstacles in our way that are contrary to the teaching you have learned. Keep away from them."

Third, treating someone as a nonbeliever may help the rebellious person to realize the seriousness of his or her sin, turn from it, and be restored to God. This third point bears repeating. The intention in treating others as nonbelievers is not to punish them but rather to help them see the seriousness of their sin and their need for repentance.

Jesus loved sinful people enough to warn them of their condition and its consequences and to urge them to repent. He said in Mark 2:17, "I have not come to call the righteous, but sinners." The church should do no less.

By God's grace, most conflicts between Christians can be resolved when a person talks personally and privately with someone who has offended him or her. When personal efforts do not succeed, Jesus has given us a simple yet effective process for involving other people who can promote understanding and agreement.

When this involvement is carried out with prayer, wisdom, and reliance on the power of the gospel, God can use our efforts to promote just settlements and preserve relationships that otherwise would be lost.

*Help me to love people enough to be an instrument in bringing them to repentance.*

## If You Are Presently Involved in a Conflict

Answering these questions will help you apply to your situation the principles presented in this week's study.

1. Are the personal or material issues in this conflict too serious to overlook or to walk away from? Why?

2. Why do you think your efforts to resolve this dispute in private have failed? Could you still do anything to resolve it in private?

3. If you must seek outside help to resolve this dispute, do you know any persons whom you and your opponent both are likely to respect and trust?

4. What will you say to your opponent to encourage him or her to allow other people to meet with the two of you to help resolve this dispute? In particular, how would you describe the advantages of gaining outside assistance?

5. If your opponent refuses to work voluntarily with others, which response would be better— dropping the matter, or asking the church to get involved? Why?

6. Go on record with the Lord by writing a prayer based on the principles contained in this lesson.

## *Week 3: Overcoming Unforgiveness*

### 1. Steps to Overcoming Unforgiveness

(1) Confirm repentance.

(2) Renounce sinful attitudes and expectations.

(3) Assess your contributions to the problem.

(4) Recognize that God is working for good.

(5) Remember God's forgiveness.

(6) Draw on God's strength.

**2. Read the following case studies. By the side of each, write the number of the step to overcoming unforgiveness that the individual can use in the situation described.**

___a. Juanita's dad wasn't around much while she and her siblings grew up. Years later, her dad sought to have a closer relationship with Juanita and her brothers and sisters. Because Dad's earlier neglect had hurt her deeply, Juanita continued to resent him even after he tried to change. She knew that the Lord had used for good some aspects of her childhood situation: she now led a support group for children from high-stress childhoods, such as hers. Many told her they were experiencing emotional healing from this group process. But Juanita found complete forgiveness of Dad to be tougher than she expected.

___b. Mrs. Holmes was a high-school teacher who seemed to have a personal vendetta against Christian students in her classes. Although Marian was a superb student, she thought Mrs. Holmes purposely gave her a low grade on a report card because Marian made her Christian convictions known. The lone low grade kept Marian from being valedictorian at graduation. For years Marian resented the ways Mrs. Holmes had harmed her. At a 10-year high-school reunion Marian's teacher shared with her that she recently had become a Christian. She asked Marian and some of the other Christian students who attended the reunion to forgive her for treating them unfairly when she taught them. Marian was still so angry about the slight to her that she could hardly look the teacher in the eye as Mrs. Holmes talked about her decision for Christ.

___c. Roger made sarcastic remarks about his co-worker, Kathy, because he thought she wasn't filling her orders quickly enough. One day his remarks were so cutting, Kathy left her work station in tears. Roger

followed Kathy to the break room. He told her he
knew he had a problem with sarcasm, that he was
sorry, and that he would do better. As Roger walked
away, Kathy fumed to herself, "Sorry, ha! Tomorrow
he'll be his same old self—abusing people with his
caustic humor."

___d. Mac continued to stew for months after Rick
apologized for failing to notify him about a committee meeting at church. The committee had counted on
Mac to give an important report at the meeting. Its
work was stymied without Mac's providing the
crucial information. Mac was humiliated. He blamed
Rick, the chairman, for not informing him of the
meeting time change. Mac harbored unforgiveness,
even though he was partly negligent in the incident.
Once he failed to receive a meeting notice, Mac erred
in not following up with Rick to doublecheck about
the meeting time.

___e. Harriet asked her sister Jane's forgiveness for
forgetting her birthday. Jane said she forgave her.
Yet when Harriet's birthday rolled around, Jane
snubbed her sister in return while continuing to
complain to others about Harriet's initial act of
forgetfulness.

___f. Alan acted hurt when his wife, Isabel, decided to
go out "with the girls" on Friday night instead of
going to a movie with him. Isabel apologized, saying,
"Oh, sorry, hon", when she saw his hurt look. Alan
replied, "That's okay; we'll go out next week." But
things really weren't okay with Alan, who continued
to feel sad about the situation. He did not think Isabel
understood how unimportant he felt when she
treated him like this.

3. **What are the three levels at which you can pursue reconciliation through the replacement principle?**

(1) Philippians 4:8 _____

_____

(2) 2 Corinthians 2:7-8 _____

_____

(3) 1 John 3:18 _____

_____

4. **After watching "Think on These Things" from** *Peacemaker Parables,* **answer these questions:**

What replacement method did Charlotte's co-worker recommend that she use in coping with her boss, Stephen, with whom she was furious?

_____

_____

What practical reason did her co-worker use for suggesting this idea to Charlotte?

_____

_____

For what spiritual reason did he recommend she do this?

_____

_____

How successful was the replacement principle in this situation?

_____

_____

5. Reflect on today's lesson. Look back at the six steps to overcoming unforgiveness (item 1). Put a check mark by the step you believe is the most difficult for you to do. Stop and pray silently that God will use that step readily the next time you find yourself hanging onto unforgiveness.

6. For further study:
   a. Read *The Peacemaker* (3d ed.) (pp. 213-223).
   b. Do the week-3 Daily Devotionals, adapted from *The Peacemaker* (pp. 101-105).
   c. Complete the chart "If You Are Presently Involved in a Conflict" (pp. 106-107).

**Devotional Readings for Week 3**

# Day 1. Getting Specific

*Today's verse: I am happy, not because you were made sorry, but because your sorrow led you to repentance (2 Cor. 7:9).*

I had told Corlette I was sorry for criticizing her in front of our neighbors. I had asked her to forgive me; she said she would.

But several hours later she still acted hurt and sad. I was friendly and warm toward her and asked her to go with me to the movies, but she refused. I tried to act light-hearted, but nothing I did put a smile on her face.

Finally, a while later, she approached me and said, "I'm having a difficult time forgiving you; could we talk about this some more?" When I agreed, she told me that she did not believe I realized how deeply I had hurt her. She then explained why my remarks had been so embarrassing and painful for her.

She was right; I had not understood the effect my words had on her.

After hearing her explanation, I confessed more specifically and sincerely for the effect my sin had on her. I committed myself to be more sensitive toward her in the future. Once I repented and confessed properly, Corlette found forgiving me to be much easier.

If you are having a difficult time forgiving someone, you may need to do what Corlette did. She helped me to see where my confession had been deficient and to take my repentance more seriously.

*Help me, Lord, to have the courage to be bold in my forgiveness—even if this means sharing my heart with the person who has wronged me.*

## Day 2. God's Instrument

*Today's verse: You intended to harm me, but God intended it for good to accomplish what is now being done (Gen. 50:20).*

When Terri arrived at work one morning, her boss summoned her. He told her, "The company is laying you off; pack your belongings; be out of the building by noon."

Fighting back tears as she threw her things in boxes, Terri burned inside. "How can he do this to me?"

A year later the boss himself was fired in an executive shake-up. He saw Terri in the grocery store and apologized to her about what had happened to her job. He claimed he had been forced to let her go. Terri thought it was a weak excuse. Several years later, Terri still harbored unforgiveness, even though God had provided a new job for her and had looked after her family in the interim.

One day a sermon touched her. The pastor urged the congregation to look on people who had wronged them as God's instruments to grow their character, enlarge their faith, point out sinful ways, and move them into situations that would glorify Him.

Terri thought seriously about what the pastor said. She realized how her old job had kept her from her family; how her time of unemployment after the layoff had caused her to totally depend on God instead of on her own capabilities; how her new job had put her in a situation to witness more and to grow as a Christian. *God has worked through the layoff and has brought me to a new level in my Christian walk because of all I have learned,* she thought.

With that new realization, Terri at last set aside years of bitter resentment and made complete forgiveness possible. As years passed, she was able to regard the painful layoff time as something God used for good.

*Nothing happen to us apart from your will, God. You are always on Your throne in the midst of our troubles. Help me to see how You work for good even in the darkest times.*

# Day 3. When God Asks the Impossible

*Today's verse: My grace is sufficient for you, for my power is made perfect in weakness (2 Cor. 12:9).*

Author Corrie ten Boom's familiar story is a splendid example of how someone painfully offended can forgive even the harshest treatment. Nazis seized her family for aiding Jews in World War II. Her father and sister died as a result of brutal abuse. Corrie wrote this about an encounter, years later, with one of her former captors:

"It was at a church service in Munich that I saw him, the former S.S. man who had stood guard at the shower room in the processing center at Ravensbruck. He was the first of our actual jailers that I had seen since that time. And suddenly it was all there—the roomful of mocking men, the heaps of clothing, Betsie's pain-blanched face.

"He came up to me as the church was emptying, beaming and bowing. 'How grateful I am for your message, Fraulein,' he said. 'To think that, as you say, he has washed my sins away!'

"His hand was thrust out to shake mine. And I, who had preached so often to the people in Bloemendall about the need to forgive, kept my hand at my side.

"I tried to smile, I struggled to raise my hand. I could not. I felt nothing, not even the slightest spark of warmth or charity. And so again I breathed a silent prayer. 'Jesus, I cannot forgive him. Give me Your forgiveness.'

"As I took his hand the most incredible thing happened. From my shoulder along my arm and through my hand a current seemed to pass from me to him, while into my heart sprang a love for this stranger that almost overwhelmed me. So I discovered that it is not on our forgiveness any more than on our goodness that the world's healing hinges, but on him. When he tells us to love our enemies, he gives, along with the command, the love itself."[1]

*Lord, we are insufficient to forgive; You are our sufficiency. Help us call on You.*

[1]Corrie ten Boom, *The Hiding Place* (New York: Bantam, 1974), 238.

## Day 4. A Lesson on the Coffee Aisle

*Today's verse: Do to others as you would have them do to you (Luke 6:31).*

Corlette and I had quarreled about some petty thing. I really had not forgiven her. I became even more resentful when she asked me to run to the grocery store to "pick up a few small items." (As you might guess from this statement, I dislike shopping for groceries.)

As I grudgingly pushed my cart down the aisle, muttering to myself all the while, I noticed some special coffee that Corlette loves to drink.

*If she hadn't been so unkind to me today, I would have surprised her with that,* I said under my breath.

Even as I thought these words, another part of me wanted to get her the coffee. For a few moments I wrestled with conflicting feelings and then decided to pick up the coffee can "just to check the price", I told myself.

The moment I touched the can, my feelings began to change. My resentment soon melted away. I was overwhelmed with love for my wife and with a desire to see her face light up as I gave her this gift.

Needless to say, Corlette and I were completely reconciled shortly after I returned home. This time, I had forgiven her not only in word but also in deed. My feelings of love followed that action of love. I thanked God for prompting me to pick up the coffee in order to experience the power of the replacement principle once more.

*By Your deeds as well as Your words, dear God, You have given us the supreme example of forgiveness. Help me to put feet to my forgiveness of others, even when my heart wants to hold on to bitterness and resentment.*

# Day 5. In Word and in Deed

*Today's verse: But I tell you who hear me: Love your enemies, do good to those who hate you, bless those who curse you, pray for those who mistreat you (Luke 6:27-28).*

In high school, best friends Bud and Todd quarreled over a girl they both wanted to date. Bud spread malicious rumors about Todd. Later he apologized. Todd said he forgave him, but when Bud encountered him at an auto-repair shop three years later and spoke warmly to Todd, Todd was aloof and walked the other way.

Years passed (incidentally, neither man married the girl!) The two men lived in different states and never encountered each other on their trips back to their hometown. Each succeeded in his vocation, each man become a parent, and each went through the sad experience of losing a parent in death. The issue which had fractured their relationship was long since forgotten in the importance of other life events.

More than 30 years after Bud and Todd graduated from high school, their paths crossed once again. Learning Bud's whereabouts, Todd called him for lunch. Bud accepted tentatively, remembering their last, unpleasant encounter. But now, Todd demonstrated true forgiveness. He told Bud he regretted being rude to him during their meeting years before. That day Todd picked up the tab for their luncheon, he asked to meet Bud's wife and children, he praised Bud to his face for his business success, and he began speaking well of Bud to others.

Todd's loving actions communicated that this time, he took the act of forgiveness seriously. He put the replacement principle into action and showed his commitment to making their relationship as good, if not better, than it was before their breach.

*Lord, help me take the bold steps of acting kindly toward all those who have wronged me and repented.*

## If You Are Presently Involved in a Conflict

Answering these questions will help you apply to your situation the principles presented in this week's study.

1. If you are having a difficult time forgiving your opponent:

    a. Is this because you are not sure he or she has repented? If so, how could you encourage confirmation of repentance?

    b. Do you think your opponent somehow must earn or deserve your forgiveness? Are you trying to punish by withholding forgiveness? Are you expecting a guarantee that the offense will not occur again? If you have any of these attitudes or expectations, what do you need to do?

    c. How did your sins contribute to this problem? Which of these sins will God refuse to forgive if you repent? How can you imitate His forgiveness?

    d. Read Matthew 18:21-35. What is the point of this passage? How does it apply to you? How might God be working for good in this situation?

e. For what has God forgiven you in the past? How serious are your opponent's sins against you when compared with your sins against God? How can you show God that you appreciate His forgiveness?

2. How can you demonstrate forgiveness or promote reconciliation

a. in thought?

b. in word?

c. in deed?

3. Go on record with the Lord by writing a prayer based on the principles this chapter teaches.

## *Week 4: Look Also to the Interests of Others*

**1. Put a star by the statement that most typifies how you regard the interests of others.**

\_\_\_\_ I'm out for Number One. Let other people take care of themselves.

\_\_\_\_ Nobody thinks about my interests. Why should I give a flip about theirs?

\_\_\_\_ If I start paying attention to the feelings and concerns of others, I'll get stepped on.

\_\_\_\_ I know the Bible tells me to take others' needs into consideration, but I've had a tough life. It's all I can do to get my own needs met.

\_\_\_\_ I'd like to know more about looking to others' interests in conflict resolution. This is an interesting concept for me. I'm sure I haven't done enough of this in the past.

**2.**               <u>**Competitive Negotiating**</u>

**Pros**                                        **Cons**

## Cooperative Negotiating

Pros                              Cons

**3. Read the following statement pertaining to the "Prepare" step in the PAUSE process:** "You can either put your time into grumbling about a problem or put that time into carefully negotiating with others. The sooner you devote your time to planning a solution to the problem, the less time you will spend stewing over it." Below, write how you feel about that statement. Do you agree or disagree? Describe your thoughts.

_____

_____

**4. In thinking about the "Affirm relationships" step in the PAUSE process, recall a time when you affirmed a relationship as you began to discuss a conflict situation. Describe what happened and how it impacted the outcome of the negotiations.**

_____

_____

**5. When negotiating, going beyond** *issues* **and** *positions* **and focusing on underlying interests is important. Fill in the blanks below based on what your leader has just told you about issues, positions, and interests.**

- An _____ is an identifiable and concrete question that must be answered to reach an agreement.
- A _____ is a desired outcome or a definable perspective on an issue.
- An _____ is what really motivates people—a concern, desire, need, value, or limitation.

**6. In your Bible read Daniel 1:11-16. Answer the following questions, based on what you read:**

What was the issue in this conflict?

_____

_____

What were the king's probable interests?

_____

_____

What were his officials' probable interests?

_____

_____

What were Daniel's interests?

_____

_____

How did Daniel objectively evaluate a possible solution?

_____

_____

**7. After again watching "Word Pictures" in** *Peacemaker Parables*, **answer these questions:**

What issue is the couple negotiating? Is it competitive or cooperative negotiation? _____

_____

What about the couple's interaction indicates that Janet prepared for her negotiation with Jim?

_____

_____

In a true cooperative negotiation situation, what interests of Jim's would Janet have attempted to understand? _____

_____

**8. For further study:**
   a. Read *The Peacemaker* (3d ed.) (pp. 225-245).
   b. Do the week-4 Daily Devotionals, adapted from *The Peacemaker* (pp. 112-116).
   c. Complete the exercise "Focusing on Interests: The Wisdom of Abigail" (p. 117).
   d. Complete "If You Are Presently Involved in a Conflict" (p. 118).

# Day 1. The Barking Dog

*Today's verse: Each of you should look not only to your own interests, but also to the interests of others (Phil. 2:4).*

Jim and Julie Johnson and Steve and Sally Smith live on nearby acreages outside of town. The Smiths, who raise border collies as a hobby and as a small business, have a new dog named Molly, who barks sporadically several evenings a week. The barking keeps the Johnsons and their children awake at night; their children complain of being tired at school. The Smiths also exercise Molly at 5 a.m., robbing the Johnsons of more sleep.

Jim, noticing Sally outdoors, asked her if she would do something about the barking. She apologized; the barking was better briefly but soon grew worse than before. Julie learned from several sources that Steve had called all the other neighbors to see whether Molly bothered them. In the process, he had criticized Jim.

Conducting her own investigation, Julie found that Molly's barking actually was bothering only a few neighbors. Two neighbors were hard of hearing; some of the others live too far away to hear the dog. The county attorney told Julie that keeping a dog that disturbs a "considerable number of people" in a neighborhood is a misdemeanor. However, he did not believe this situation qualified, since few were bothered.

With this information in hand, Jim and Julie saw that they would need to negotiate a solution without the aid of authorities. They began praying, asking God for wisdom and discernment in a matter that could well interfere with neighborly goodwill if not settled harmoniously.

*Lord, sometimes the easiest thing for me to do when I don't get my way is to bottle up my anger or blow up. Yet, I know that this is not Your way. Help me to act Christlike when I'm in conflict.*

# Day 2. Pausing to Prepare

*Today's verse: [Love] is not self-seeking (1 Cor. 13:5).*

Jim and Julie decided to prepare carefully before negotiating with the Smiths. They began writing down times when Molly barked. Jim learned that their subdivision had no rules against barking dogs. Julie also read books explaining expert trainers' suggestions on barking dogs.

They identified issues to be addressed. Their interests included a desire for peace and quiet and sufficient rest for their children. The Smiths' interests, they speculated, were a love for dogs and a need for extra income. Additionally, perhaps they resented being told what to do.

The Johnsons then thought of options to solve the problem, such as selling the dog, muzzling the dog, or getting ear plugs for themselves or a remote-controlled shock collar for Molly. They anticipated how the Smiths would react to each option and possible costs involved.

They strategized what to do if the Smiths refused to act. Although they were tempted to retaliate, they knew this would not honor God. The Johnsons knew they could work more diligently at getting to know the Smiths and their children and look for chances to be kind to them.

The Johnsons decided to approach the Smiths on a Saturday, since Steve and Sally seemed to relax more then. They also planned for the meeting to be at the Smith home, to put the Smiths at ease.

Once their preparations were complete, Jim and Julie were ready to approach the Smiths. Only time would tell whether their relationships would forever be impaired or strengthened by how they approached this conflict.

*Help me to try to see things through other peoples' eyes, Lord. Help me to pray for those who oppose me.*

## Day 3. Conveying Courtesy

*Today's verse: Pleasant words are a honeycomb, sweet to the soul and healing to the bones (Prov. 16:24).*

Soon Jim went to the Smiths' home and said, "Molly seems to be barking a lot lately. Our children are having a difficult time getting enough sleep. Julie and I would appreciate your taking a few minutes to talk with us about the situation." Affirming their relationship with the Smiths was a basic part of the Johnsons' approach. By asking for a meeting instead of demanding it, Jim conveyed courtesy and respect.

The process continued during their first meeting with the Smiths the next day. Jim began by saying, "We appreciate your willingness to talk with us. In fact, we hope this situation will give us a chance to get to know each other better and be better neighbors than before."

Julie asked for permission to explain some of her and Jim's concerns. Using "I" and "we" statements instead of the accusatory "you", Julie was careful not to accuse the Smiths of deliberately bothering anyone and clearly indicated that she and Jim were assuming the best about them. She then asked Steve and Sally to explain some of their feelings and concerns. As they did so, Jim and Julie asked questions at appropriate times and responded with statements such as, "I see", "I didn't realize that", and "That helps me to understand your situation."

Although the Smiths were somewhat defensive when the conversation began, they eventually began to relax. As their relationship with the Johnsons was affirmed, they became increasingly willing to talk about the problem that had brought them together.

*Dear God, help us turn conflicts into growth situations for ourselves and those with whom we disagree.*

# Day 4. Thinking Creatively

*Today's verse: A man of knowledge uses words with restraint, and a man of understanding is even-tempered (Prov. 17:27).*

Continuing to talk, the Johnsons suggested that they try to understand each others' interests in the barking-dog situation. Steve and Sally immediately stated that they would not get rid of Molly. Jim responded, "You value her a lot, don't you?" The Johnsons' paraphrasing of the Smiths' further comments showed they were truly listening. They learned more of the Smiths' interests. Molly was descended from one of Sally's father's favorite dogs. Molly's barking at disturbances reassured them because their house once was burglarized. Steve felt great success as a breeder and trainer despite his disappointment in his accounting job.

As Jim and Julie listened, they realized the Smiths would not consider getting rid of Molly. They knew this called for some creative thinking.

As they brainstormed (the Smiths had relaxed as they saw the Johnsons being reasonable), Sally suggested that they consider times Molly barked most—times the Smiths were out of town and Molly had not been exercised. Julie offered for their daughter, Karen, to walk Molly daily when the Johnsons were gone. They then discussed whether Molly was barking at people walking along a nearby highway. Could Steve move the kennel away from the highway? Steve replied that he didn't have time, that hiring someone would be costly, and that the dogs would be too hot away from the present, shady location.

Jim saw that Steve was growing impatient, so he suggested that they think about things for a few days and meet again.

*Nothing is too insignificant to pray about, Lord. Help me turn every matter in my life, both large and small, over to you. I know you care.*

## Day 5. Good Solutions, Good Friends

*Today's verse: Do not cause anyone to stumble, whether Jews, Greeks or the church of God (1 Cor. 10:32).*

Back home, the Johnsons kept a journal of Molly's barking. The barking episodes clearly coincided with people riding or walking by on the highway. By Jim and Julie's next meeting with the Smiths, they had gathered objective information as well as some creative proposals.

Seeing the Johnsons' journal, Steve still was defensive. Molly might be barking at people, but he still didn't have time or money to move the kennel, especially away from shade. Jim countered by suggesting that he and his son, who needed construction experience, help Steve move the kennel. He also offered Steve dozens of young trees that grew on his father-in-law's property. The trees would shade the kennel.

Jim's proposal was so reasonable that Steve couldn't think of how to say no. Then Julie again offered Karen's services to walk Molly. She acknowledged Sally's reluctance to trust her dogs to a stranger and suggested that Karen work alongside Sally for a week to learn care of the dogs. Julie said Karen didn't expect pay but might enjoy having a puppy out of Molly's next litter.

Once the conversation turned to puppies, Steve warmed to Jim and Julie's suggestions. The details took a while to work out, but the experience eventually made the families better neighbors and friends.

Jim and Julie were thankful for the outcome because they knew that as they dealt with their neighbors, they were representing Christ. How would Christ look to those with whom you deal in a conflict?

*Lord, I'm a walking, talking representative of You here on earth as I go about my dealings with other people. Help others see You in the way I act during the tough times.*

## Focusing on Interests: The Wisdom of Abigail

**Read 1 Samuel 25:1-44 in your Bible. Answer the following questions about this passage, which is one of the most effective uses of negotiation in Scripture.**

What did Nabal do that angered David?

_____

_____

What was David's reaction?

_____

_____

What did Abigail do to prepare for her meeting with David?

_____

_____

How did she affirm her concern and respect for David?

_____

_____

On what interest of David did she focus?

_____

_____

How did David respond?

_____

_____

### If You Are Presently Involved in a Conflict

Answering these questions will help you apply to your situation the principles presented in this week's study.

1. Which style of negotiation is most appropriate in your situation: competitive or cooperative? Why?

2. How can you prepare to negotiate a reasonable agreement in this situation?

3. How can you affirm your concern and respect for your opponent?

4. Understand the interests by answering these questions:
   a. Which material issues need to be resolved in order to settle this conflict? What positions have you and your opponent already taken on these issues?

   b. What are your interests in this situation?

   c. What are your opponent's interests in this situation?

5. What are some creative solutions or options that would satisfy as many interests as possible?

6. What are some ways that these options can be evaluated objectively and reasonably?

7. Go on record with the Lord by writing a prayer based on the principles this chapter teaches.

## *Week 5: Overcome Evil with Good*

1. At this point in the study, my largest, ongoing challenge in being a peacemaker is:

_____

_____

2. Look up the Scripture passages listed below. In the right-hand column list one divine weapon that the passage mentions that we have as Christians to use (as opposed to the ways the world offers) in our quest for peace.

Luke 6:27-28, 35-36          _____

2 Corinthians 10:5          _____

2 Corinthians 5:18          _____

Galatians 5:22-23          _____

Romans 12:14          _____

John 14:15-17          _____

### 3. Fill in the blanks of the following statement:

Realizing who we are in Christ inspires us to do the unnatural work of dying to _____, confessing _____, addressing _____ graciously, laying down _____, and forgiving _____—even with people who persist in opposing or mistreating us.

### 4. List the five steps to overcoming evil—
   • Control your _____.
   • Seek godly _____.
   • Keep doing what is _____.
   • Recognize your _____.
   • Use the _____ weapon.

### 5. Beside each case study listed below write one of the five principles that contributes to a victorious offensive that the person uses in the vignette.

_____ 1. Greta's co-worker, Jim, goaded her into a fight over which of them would work overtime at the plant on the night shift. As discussions grew heated, Greta called Jim lazy and uncooperative. Later she apologized to Jim; they worked out an arrangement for the night shift. But the damage was done. In front of others Jim continued to make sarcastic remarks about Greta. Greta kept her promise to herself to be unfailingly cheerful and friendly with Jim despite his hurtful remarks. She spoke kindly to him and tried to avoid getting dragged down again by his bad attitude.

_____ 2. The new mission church had met in a day-care center for more than a year. Although the relationship between the church and Pat, the day-care center director, had started out peaceably enough, in time Pat became more and more demanding and picky about rules for maintaining the center. Eventually she asked Pastor Sam to find another location for the mission. Pastor Sam apologized to Pat for the troubles she cited and offered to make any repairs she felt necessary. Pat merely mumbled something and did not accept the pastor's offer. In the community she made many negative comments about the church. On the last day the church met in the center, Pastor Sam asked Pat to be present. He presented her with a plaque, a floral arrangement, and a check to paint the center in gratitude for the mission church's being allowed to meet there for the past year.

_____ 3. In a bitter court battle Mariana lost custody of her daughter. On weekends that the girl visited her mom, she complained of conditions in her father's home, where she had to share with three older siblings from her father's new marriage. During the week, when Mariana telephoned her daughter, her ex-husband refused to let the two of them speak to each other. Many friends and co-workers urged Mariana to fight her ex in court over the situation. Her pastor made a counterproposal: In six months her daughter would be old enough to tell the judge she wanted to return to her mother's home. He encouraged Mariana to treat her ex as civilly and courteously as possible during their interactions and to wait for the moment when life circumstances could change naturally.

_____ 4. Doug's brother unexpectedly jumped on him one day about grudges and grievances that he had held against Doug from their childhoods. The discussion was public, in front of other family members. Although caught off-guard and thoroughly surprised at Bill's suppressed anger toward him, Doug did the best he could to apologize specifically for each of Bill's complaints and told Bill that he wanted to restore goodwill between them. Doug did his best to put the hurtful discussion behind him and to restore cordial relations, but whenever he was with Bill, Bill continued to act hostile. Privately, Doug continued to pray for Bill and to ask God to intervene to help Bill accept Doug's apology.

_____ 5. Phyllis was in charge of Christmas decorations for her street. Neighbors in six of the seven homes on the *cul-de-sac* willingly agreed to work one Saturday to hang greenery on the street-entrance signs and to put out sacks with candles in front of each house. The exception was Dave, the former decorations chairman, who resented Phyllis' being in charge instead of him. Dave left for the bowling alley on the Saturday when everyone turned out to work. Several neighbors suggested that they leave Dave's house without sacks and candles in exchange for his unhelpfulness. Phyllis refused to act vindictive. She spent her own money to buy the necessary items to decorate Dave's curbside as well.

**6. After again watching "Why Not Rather Be Wronged?" from *Peacemaker Parables*, answer these questions:**

Which of the five godly principles discussed in this lesson was Scott following in dealing with the lawsuit?

_____

_____

Why did his attorney fail to understand when Scott spoke about wanting a clean conscience?

_____

_____

What word picture did Scott paint in talking about his outlook on dropping the case?

_____

_____

How difficult would taking a costly stand, as Scott did, be for you? Why?

_____

_____

**7. For further study:**
   a. Read *The Peacemaker* (3d ed.) (pp. 247-256).
   b. Do the week-5 Daily Devotionals, adapted from *The Peacemaker* (pp. 123-127).
   c. Complete "If You Are Presently Involved in a Conflict" (pp. 128-129).

# Day 1. The High Road

*Today's verse: For we are taking pains to do what is right, not only in the eyes of the Lord but also in the eyes of men (2 Cor. 8:21).*

When John's wife, Karen, divorced him and moved in with her high-school sweetheart, John was devastated, especially when his church refused to do anything to try to save their marriage.

But he drew on God's grace and resisted the temptation to give in to self-pity or bitterness. He refused to criticize Karen, especially in front of their children. He bent over backward to accommodate their ever-changing visitation schedule. Most of all, he continued to pray for Karen. When they talked with each other, he asked God to help him speak to her with genuine love and gentleness.

After a year, Karen and her boyfriend were fighting continually. As she compared his behavior to John's unfailing kindness in the face of her betrayal, she began to realize her terrible mistake. With great trepidation she asked John if any chance existed that they could get together again. To her amazement, John said yes and suggested that they start counseling with the pastor at John's new church. Eight months later, their children had the joy of seeing their parents renew their vows and reunite their family.

Whether Karen returned to him or not, John's decision to keep doing what was right honored God. His behavior also was a powerful witness to his children about Christ's love and forgiveness. He later learned that his example had helped some other divorced people to respond to their ex-spouses graciously, even though none of their marriages were restored. As John demonstrated, doing what is right—even in the face of unjust treatment—is always the safest path to walk.

*Help me to take the high road in relating to those who hurt me.*

## Day 2. Ending the Freeze-Out

*Today's verse: Love is not rude, it is not self-seeking, it is not easily angered, it keeps no record of wrongs (1 Cor. 13:5).*

In some cases, God may use our loving acts to soften the hearts of our opponents. I am blessed to have a wife who, time after time, has loved me like this.

One night we had such a strong disagreement that we went to bed unreconciled. (Yes, we broke the command not to let the sun go down on our anger.) As we lay there facing away from each other, a bizarre contest developed. Without a word, we tacitly agreed that "he who moves first is weak." I was not going to budge an inch until Corlette moved. She was just as determined not to move until I did. So we lay there like two frozen bodies.

I soon was more frozen than I wanted to be. I had been so distracted when I crawled into bed that I had not pulled the covers over me. We usually slept with our bedroom window open, but the weather had turned cold. The room soon was very cold, as was I. But I was so caught up in my stubborn pride that I refused to move and pull up the covers.

After a few minutes, I began to tremble from the cold. Corlette felt it through the mattress and slowly turned her head (so I could not tell she was moving!) to see what was going on. She understood my predicament: her silly, stubborn husband had backed himself into a corner and needed help to get out. Giving up her desire to win the ridiculous contest of wills, Corlette made the first move. She reached down, took hold of the blankets at my feet, and pulled them gently over my shoulders.

In a few moments I was trembling even more but not from the cold. Her loving gesture was so entirely undeserved that it broke my heart. My anger and pride dissolved. With tears of regret I turned to Corlette and experienced the joy and freedom derived from making peace.

*Father, help me know the joy that stems from humbling myself and living peaceably.*

# Day 3. In the Face of Evil

*Today's verse: The Lord detests the way of the wicked but he loves those who pursue righteousness (Prov. 15:9).*

Ernest Gordon's marvelous book, *To End All Wars* (formerly titled *Through the Valley of the Kwai*), describes the power of loving an enemy. During World War II the Japanese captured Gordon and forced him, with other British prisoners, to endure horrible treatment while building the notorious "Railroad of Death" through Thailand. Faced with the starvation and disease of the prison camps and the brutality of his captors, who killed hundreds of his comrades, Gordon survived to become an inspiring example of the triumph of Christian love against human evil.

This love shone especially bright one day when Gordon and his fellow prisoners found a trainload of wounded Japanese soldiers who were being transported to Bangkok. Abandoned and with no one to care for them, these soldiers had inflamed, bloody, pus-infested wounds that oozed onto their uniforms. Their faces bore hopeless looks as they waited for death. No wonder, Gordon noted, that the Japanese treated their prisoners so cruelly—they had no regard for their own people.

Gordon recalled how, wordlessly, most of the officers in his section took out rags, rations, and water canteens and boarded the Japanese train to aid the wounded men. His colleagues ignored their own guards' warnings and knelt by the enemy to administer help and say a kind word. As they left, they heard the Japanese soldiers cry out, "*Aragatto!*" ("Thank you!")[1]

Most of us never will be subjected to this kind of abuse or have to reach across so great a chasm to love those who have wronged us. Keep stories such as Ernest Gordon's in mind when you are challenged to love an enemy.

*How can I love in the face of abuse and insensitivity? Only by your grace, Lord. Please enable me.*

[1] Ernest Gordon, *To End All Wars* (Grand Rapids: Zondervan, 2002), 197-8.

## Day 4. The Battle Is Not Yours

*Today's verse: For evil men will be cut off, but those who hope in the Lord will inherit the land (Ps. 37:9).*

Even before he hired her, Sarah's boss affirmed her abilities. Once she joined his company, the boss regularly gave Sarah outstanding merit reviews and pay raises. She, likewise, became his ardent supporter and worked diligently on projects he assigned. When she overheard co-workers disparage the boss, she publicly defended him.

One day, however, the boss inexplicably turned on Sarah. She learned that he instigated negative peer reviews of her among the employees she managed. In a staff meeting he made rude remarks about her. When Sarah visited her boss to inquire why she had fallen from his favor, her boss demoted her and reduced her salary. To avoid further humiliation, Sarah resigned. She was totally defeated by these bewildering events.

As a Christian, Sarah pled with God to punish her former employer who had acted unjustly. After leaving the company, Sarah continued to hear how he similarly mistreated other employees. She begged God to intervene, not only on her behalf but also on behalf of all those likewise maligned. Months passed; Sarah saw no sign of answered prayer. Other injured former workers wanted her to join them in slander campaigns against the boss. Sarah declined, believing God would someday deal in His own way with this. Meanwhile, He blessed Sarah and prospered her in a new job. He took care of her family and gave her peace about her past, work-related trauma.

Years later, the day arrived when the former boss finally made too many enemies. His supervisors created a low-level desk job for him at which he could obscurely coast to retirement but no longer harm employees. In His time and way, God punished this unrepentant, cruel boss while he blessed Sarah for her faithfulness.

*Lord, I wait for Your promised delivery from my enemies.*

# Day 5. High-Profile Control

*Today's verse: We work hard with our own hands. When we are cursed, we bless; when we are persecuted, we endure it. (1 Cor. 4:12).*

Charlie, a Christian, was mayor of his town. Charlie began some innovative programs for his community. He wanted to restore the historic downtown area, attract new businesses, and improve housing for minorities. While some residents supported his far-reaching programs, others wanted the town to stay "the way it's always been."

Charlie's proposals—and the opposition to them—generated widespread media attention. Many opponents approached area newspapers and television stations. Their one-sided, distorted version of the story drew interest from some reporters. One particularly forceful opponent was the adult daughter of a former mayor. Although the two families once had been friends, the daughter now led the pack of opposition against Charlie. She went on the warpath and rounded up others to approach news media members and attack Charlie. Many of the attacks resulted in bitter, unfair, public character assassinations.

Through the ordeal, Charlie impressed many with his unfailing control over his tongue. Despite his opponents' malicious attacks, he responded only in a kindly, gracious fashion—speaking only to the issues instead of to the personal assaults. When reporters asked Charlie why he didn't fire back, Charlie credited God's strength and attributed the prayers of his family and friends for helping him maintain a loving attitude toward his enemies.

Charlie narrowly escaped defeat in the next mayoral race. His enemies vowed to continue to fight him on every front throughout his new term. But those whose hearts he had won thanked God for this Christian role model who took seriously the biblical admonition to avoid repaying evil with evil or insult with insult.

*Help me remember, O Father, that others watch how I react in the midst of conflict. Keep my witness strong.*

## If You Are Presently Involved in a Conflict

If you are presently involved in a conflict, these questions will help you to apply the principles this chapter presents.

1. On whom are you relying to guide your responses to this conflict?

2. Which worldly weapons have you been using, or are you tempted to use, in this situation?

3. How can the gospel of Jesus Christ guide, motivate, and empower you from this point forward?

4. Have you been using your tongue to bless your opponents—or to speak critically of them? How could you breathe grace in the days ahead?

5. To whom can you turn for godly advice and encouragement?

6. What can you keep on doing in this situation that is right?

7. Have you done everything in your power to live at peace with your opponent? Is turning to church or civil authorities appropriate to seek assistance in resolving this dispute?

8. What needs does your opponent have that God may want you to try to meet? In other words, how can you love your opponent in a deliberate and focused way?

9. Go on record with the Lord by writing a prayer based on the principles this chapter teaches.

# Week 6: Cultivating a Culture of Peace in Your Church

**1. List four benefits that spring to your mind about ways a church would benefit from its members becoming peacemakers, or cultivating "a culture of peace."**

a. _____

b. _____

c. _____

d. _____

**2. Fill in the blanks in the following definition of a "culture of peace."**

A culture of peace is the combination of _____, _____, _____, and _____ for resolving conflict.

**3. Based on the levels you just heard described, put a check by the level of peacemaking you believe your own church has reached at this time.**

Level 1—A Culture of Disbelief
Level 2—A Culture of Faith
Level 3—A Culture of Transformation
Level 4—A Culture of Peace
Level 5—A Culture of Multiplication

If you did not indicate that your church is at level 5, what do you think would be required for your church to reach a higher level?

_____
_____
_____
_____

4.          **Characteristics of a Culture of Peace**

**In the blanks that follow write which of the eight characteristics of a culture of peace—assistance, training, stability, witness, restoration, perseverance, vision, accountability—the verses after the blank describe.**

a. _____ (see Luke 6:27-36; John 13:35; 1 Cor. 10:31; Col. 3:12-14).
b. _____ (see Gal. 5:19-21; Luke 6:40; Eph. 4:24-26; 1 Tim. 4:15-16; Titus 2:1-10).
c. _____ (see Matt. 18:16; Rom. 15:14; 1 Cor. 6:1-8; Gal. 6:1-2; Col. 3:16).
d. _____ (see Matt. 18:12-16; 19:1-9; Rom. 12:18; Eph. 4:1-3; Matt. 19:1-9; 1 Cor. 7:1-11).
e. _____ (see Prov. 3:11-12; Matt. 18:12-20; 1 Cor. 5:1-5; Jas. 5:19-20).
f. _____ (see Matt. 18:21-35; Eph. 4:32; 2 Cor. 2:5-11).
g. _____ (see 1 Tim. 4:15; Heb. 10:25).
h. _____ (see Matt. 5:9; John 13:34-35; 17:20-23; 1 Pet. 2:12; 3:15-16).

**5. Why is what Christ has done for you motivation to adopt a culture of peace?**

_____
_____
_____

**6. What could your group do collectively to help bring about a culture of peace in your church?**

_____

_____

_____

_____

_____

_____

_____

**7. Think about how you can react to the lesson's statement, "The only thing necessary is for one person to hear the call of God and respond, 'Here am I. Send me!' (Isa. 6:8)." What do you intend to do individually to help your church become a "peacemaking church" and to adopt a culture of peace?**

_____

_____

_____

**8. After watching "Peacemaker Junkie" from _Peacemaker Parables_, answer these questions:**

What underlying message does Ted attempt to convey as he checks in with the Peacemakers Anonymous group?

_____

_____

What did Ted really mean when he said he wanted to "live like a zombie again" and "get back to normal Christianity again"?

_____

_____

**9. For further study:**
   a. Read _The Peacemaker_ (3d ed.) (pp. 289-297).
   b. Do the week-6 Daily Devotionals, adapted from _The Peacemaker_ (pp. 133-137).

# Day 1. This Old House

*Today's verse: Whoever loves God must also love his brother
(1 John 4:21).*

The large, suburban church was situated in a neighborhood of vintage homes. Years ago, one of the homes—the Grey family's home—had been deeded to the church to use as a temporary residence for visiting clergy and church guests. However, the church and the Grey heirs had been at odds for years. As a result, the heirs hesitated to totally vacate the property so that the church could take possession.

In the stalemate, the house sat unoccupied. Neighbors grew concerned about safety, especially when they saw gangs from the nearby high school gather on the darkened front porch at night. Students on their way to school smoked as they hid behind storage buildings on the property. Neighbors worried about possible fires.

People in the neighborhood looked to the church to intervene. But when neighbors voiced concerns, one of the elderly church leaders remarked, "They ought to just tear it down and build a parking lot and end the whole ruckus." Naturally, this remark made the neighbors angry and fearful about what might happen on their street.

One family in the neighborhood was unchurched. Although a member occasionally invited this family to attend, the husband replied, "I'll never go to that church because of the bad example it sets in the neighborhood."

The church had a responsibility to be a good neighbor, but its witness was being tarnished by the dispute over the house. The conflict was ripe for a peacemaking opportunity. But how could the situation be resolved after many years of being on dead center?

*Lord, my actions influence many around me. Help me remember that I'm Your representative.*

## Day 2. A Sticky Wicket

*Today's verse: Let this mind be in you, which was also in Christ Jesus (Phil. 2:5 KJV).*

Jake and his family lived in one of the restored, older homes on the same street with the Grey home. As a church member, Jake knew how frustrated the church was not to be able to use the house because of the donor family's hesitation. He knew how much the church needed the home for long-awaited, church-guest housing.

Yet he also understood the Grey family heirs' feeling that they had been treated rudely by the church and felt that their generous donation was unappreciated. He himself had overheard one of church leaders say, "If the pastor would let me, I would go over and kick those folks out on their ear." He knew the rancor that existed on the church's side.

Jake had even overheard some members suggest that the church should sue to force the Grey family to vacate. He knew that this would be a terrible example to people who were watching to see how Christians deal with conflict. How could a win-win solution be achieved?

Jake began by asking the church to allow him to be the go-between in the conflict. Although he was not a native to the community, his wife's family had been long-time friends of the now-deceased, original owners. He hoped that this enduring relationship would help generate goodwill that would be necessary to negotiate a settlement.

When he first approached the Grey family members by phone, Jake immediately heard an earful about how insensitive and difficult the church had been. Clearly emotions, Jake saw, ran high on both sides.

Yet somehow, he sensed that more to the story had to exist than simply the fact of these two parties fighting against each other. Jake believed that if he could somehow uncover the root of the discord, this might hold the key to eventual progress.

*Help me proceed with Your wisdom when I set out to resolve a conflict.*

# Day 3. A Clue among the Discards

*Today's verse: Live as children of light (Eph. 5:8b).*

One Saturday afternoon Jake and his wife, Karen, noticed a car parked in the driveway of the Grey house. They saw that Jim and Barbara Grey, one of the heirs and his wife, were visiting the property. They strolled down the street, opened the door, and called out a cheery, "Hello!" The Greys invited the couple in. What Jake and his wife saw amazed them. In the center of each room of the home was a pile of objects—items that the Greys were considering discarding. They ranged from old clothes and hats to kitchen utensils to Christmas decorations to assorted bric-a-brac. As they made small talk with Jake and Karen, the couple paced around one pile, moved into another room, and paced around the pile of objects there.

Since Karen had visited in the home when she was a child, she mentioned recognizing one of the small, wooden shelves that lay in the center of one of the piles. Jim warmed to her comment. "Would you like to have it as a souvenir?" he asked Karen. "I couldn't," she replied modestly. "It belongs to your family." "Please," was Jim's answer. "You'd be doing us a tremendous favor. In fact," he went on, "please look in all these rooms. Take what you'd like.""Okay, maybe one more memento," she acquiesced. Barbara looked her straight in the eye and said, "No, we're serious. Take ANYTHING you want. Our children have taken their keepsakes. We've donated some valuables to museums. We can't even think of what to do with all that remains. We work here week after week, but we still can't get things cleaned out." Barbara's voice sounded weary. "We don't want to throw these family things away. We feel stuck."

Jake's ears perked up. Could this be a clue to the squabble between the church and the heirs? He felt sure something was driving the frustration there.

*Dear God, things are not always as they seem. When conflict arises, help me to look below the surface for answers.*

## Day 4. Speeding along the Exit

*Today's verse: And over all these virtues put on love, which binds them all together in perfect unity (Col. 3:14).*

"You sound very frustrated," Jake remarked to Barbara after she told Karen to keep looking through the discards.

"They don't understand," Barbara sniffed, becoming a little tearful a she spoke. "We're moving as fast as we can to get out of this house. But these items—they're the last earthly reminders we have of Grandma and Grandpa."

Jake merely nodded sympathetically and let Barbara go on. The "they" to whom she referred clearly were members of the church. "They thought that the house was given to them immediately by our family. They got mad when we didn't let them right on in. But it was deeded as part of a life estate. As long as Grandma was alive, the family continued to have possession. Only when Grandma died a year ago did they legally have a right to be here. We've been working to get it ready, but I've been recovering from surgery. I get very tired after working only briefly."

Karen touched Barbara's arm compassionately. "This must be difficult for you," Karen told her. "I'm sorry."

Then Karen hit on an idea. "Would this help? When you truly have taken all you want, Jake and I'll be happy to come in and box up the rest. Perhaps having someone else do this job would be easier. I know a little resale shop that sells discards to benefit poor people in town. I can take in items that might sell. That way your family's things can be used to help others."

Karen doubted that Barbara would go for the idea, but she leapt immediately. "Oh, would you? That would be a huge relief." "Our pleasure," Karen answered. Jake chimed in, "Then when we're finished, we'll be happy to get the home cleaned up for you. That way you don't have to tire yourself out." Jim looked genuinely touched. "Thank you," was all he could manage.

*Sometimes we make things too difficult, Lord. Please point us to an easier way.*

# Day 5. A "Win-Win" for All

*Today's verse: For he himself is our peace, who has made the two one and has destroyed the barrier, the dividing wall of hostility (Eph. 2:14).*

Progress on the Grey home wasn't instant, but it was steady from this point on. The Greys kept their word. As soon as Jake and Karen removed the last box of belongings and cleaned up the home, the Greys turned the house over to the church and went on with their lives. The church began making necessary repairs and readied the Grey home to welcome the first visiting preacher.

Because of Jake and Karen, who represented the church in the conflict resolution, the Greys went away feeling better about the church's occupancy. The neighbors were thrilled to see the home freshly painted and revitalized, with temporary residents about to occupy the place. And, of course, the church was delighted to see its long-term dream of a church guest-home come true.

Just before the first guests arrived, Jake and Karen spearheaded an open house, so that neighbors and church members alike could see the beautifully restored old home. At the open house, the church conducted a ceremony to formally thank Jim and Barbara and the rest of the Grey family for their generous donation. Then, when a guest pastor visited, the neighbors held a dessert party and invited the church guests to meet folks on the block.

Interestingly, the unchurched neighbor who had been so turned off by the church's bickering with the family paid close attention to the way the church resolved the issue. Jake and Karen hoped that in recent weeks he had seen better examples of members' Christianity.

Because one couple took on themselves the peacemaking task in a long-standing squabble, a "win-win" solution resulted. But profiting most was the cause of Christ, Whose peace shone through in this incident.

*You are pleased with us, Father, when we demonstrate Your peace. Help us to do that in every instance.*

# HOW TO FIND
# NEW LIFE IN CHRIST

No matter who you are—what job you hold, how much (or how little) money you have, what you have achieved—you are powerless over one thing—going to heaven on your own strength. God is the power source for salvation to all who believe.

We need God's power because we are all lost in sin. "For all have sinned and fall short of the glory of God" (Rom. 3:23).

A penalty exists for that sin. "For the wages of sin is death" (Rom. 6:23).

By good deeds, you cannot earn a way to wipe out that sin from your life. "For it is by grace you have been saved, through faith—and this is not from yourselves; it is the gift of God—not by works, so that no one can boast" (Eph. 2:8-9).

God provided for your sin when he sent His Son to die in your place. Instead of you, Jesus took the wages of sin on Himself by dying on the cross. Then God raised Him on the third day. "But God demonstrates his own love for us in this: While we were still sinners, Christ died for us" (Rom. 5:8).

You can claim this free gift of salvation by calling on Him. "Everyone who calls on the name of the Lord will be saved" (Rom. 10:13).

If you would like to have salvation in Jesus Christ, sincerely pray a prayer such as this one: "Dear God, I confess to You my sin and my need for salvation. I turn away from my sin and place my faith in Jesus as my Savior and Lord. Amen."

Now, find a pastor or Christian friend to tell about your decision.

Order *Member Book*, *Leader Guide*, video, trade book

# *Peacefakers, Peacebreakers, and Peacemakers*

**Call Now: 1-800-747-0738**
**Visit: www.hannibalbooks.com**
FAX: 1-888-252-3022
Email: orders@hannibalbooks.com
Mail copy of form below to:
Hannibal Books
P.O. Box 461592
Garland, Texas 75046

| | | |
|---|---|---|
| *Member Book* | _____ X $7.95 = | _____ |
| *Leader Guide* | _____ X $8.95 = | _____ |
| **Video** | _____ X $19.95 = | _____ |
| *DVD* | _____ X $29.95 = | _____ |
| *The Peacemaker*, **Third Edition** | _____ X $14.95 = | _____ |
| *Leader Kit* (**all the above except DVD**) | _____ X $45.00 = | _____ |
| *Leader Kit* (**all the above except video**) | _____ X $50.00 = | _____ |

**Total Cost:  $**_____

**Add $3 for shipping first item and 50-cents for each additional item.**
**Shipping    $**_____
**Texas residents add 8.25 % sales tax $**_____

**Total order  $**_____

**Mark method of payment:**
Check enclosed _____
Credit card# _____
        exp. date_____
(Visa, MasterCard, Discover, American Express accepted)

Name _____

Address _____

City State, Zip _____

Phone _____ FAX _____

Email _____